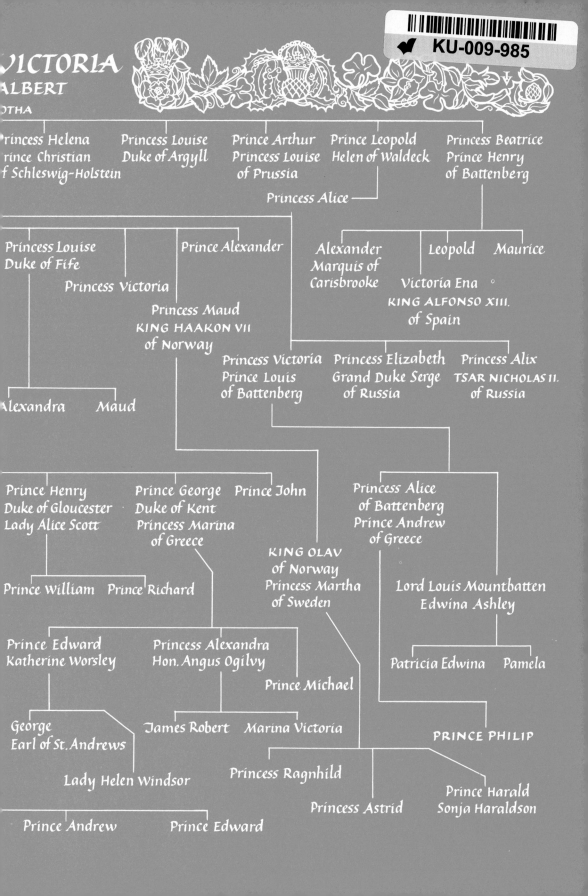

VICTORIA
ALBERT
OTHA

Princess Helena
Prince Christian
of Schleswig-Holstein

Princess Louise
Duke of Argyll

Prince Arthur
Princess Louise
of Prussia

Prince Leopold
Helen of Waldeck

Princess Beatrice
Prince Henry
of Battenberg

Princess Alice

Princess Louise
Duke of Fife

Prince Alexander

Alexander
Marquis of
Carisbrooke

Leopold   Maurice

Princess Victoria

Victoria Ena
KING ALFONSO XIII.
of Spain

Princess Maud
KING HAAKON VII
of Norway

Princess Victoria
Prince Louis
of Battenberg

Princess Elizabeth
Grand Duke Serge
of Russia

Princess Alix
TSAR NICHOLAS II.
of Russia

Alexandra   Maud

Prince Henry
Duke of Gloucester
Lady Alice Scott

Prince George
Duke of Kent
Princess Marina
of Greece

Prince John

Princess Alice
of Battenberg
Prince Andrew
of Greece

KING OLAV
of Norway
Princess Martha
of Sweden

Prince William   Prince Richard

Lord Louis Mountbatten
Edwina Ashley

Prince Edward
Katherine Worsley

Princess Alexandra
Hon. Angus Ogilvy

Prince Michael

Patricia Edwina   Pamela

George
Earl of St. Andrews

James Robert   Marina Victoria

PRINCE PHILIP

Lady Helen Windsor

Princess Ragnhild

Prince Harald
Sonja Haraldson

Princess Astrid

Prince Andrew   Prince Edward

ELIZABETH
Our Queen

ELIZABETH
Our Queen

REGINALD DAVIS

COLLINS
St James's Place, London

William Collins Sons & Co Ltd
London · Glasgow · Sydney · Auckland
Toronto · Johannesburg

First published 1976
© Reginald Davis 1976
ISBN 0 00 211233 7
Set in Monophoto Plantin
Book designed by Colin E. Reed
Colour separations by F. E. Burman Ltd
Printed and bound in Great Britain by
Jarrold and Sons Ltd, Norwich

To my wife Audrey
with whose help all things are possible

Contents

Foreword BY SIR ROBERT MENZIES

I have had the privilege of serving under four Monarchs. Under the last two, I have been a Member of the Privy Council or, as they say in the lovely language of the Summons, of the Meeting of 'the Crown's Servants'.

As for Her Majesty The Queen, she is the successor of monarchs who, in this century, have, by their own conduct and their own statements, helped to preserve our monarchy in a world in which Crowns have tumbled and disasters have beset mankind.

As a veteran servant of Her Majesty, and as one who first met her and knew her when she was a young girl, I rejoice year by year in her authority, wisdom and judgment, in her capacity to evoke feelings not only of respect, but of the warmest affection.

Rooted as the Queen's Office is in the deep soil of history, enduring as it has proved through the great shocks of political and military and social events, it enjoys the respect of all but a handful of her people. The Queen is seen in all countries within her allegiance as the fountain of honour, the protector of the law, the centre of the parliamentary system in which she proclaims statutes 'by and with the advice and consent' of Parliament. It is quite true that these things are, in a sense, a matter of form, but to those with imagination, they remain a matter of immense and lasting perpetuity.

It is a great privilege indeed, to offer a few words by way of introduction to a volume which will commemorate what I believe to be one of the greatest reigns of history. It is not for nothing that the Queen is Elizabeth II. She does great honour to her name, and I believe she has given an enduring service to the Crown, to the Monarchy, something that will be remembered and remembered with affection for all time.

ROBERT MENZIES

Melbourne,
17th March, 1976

Author's Introduction

It is twenty-five years since the young Princess Elizabeth became Elizabeth II, and despite the many thousands of times I have photographed her I still find each occasion tremendously exciting.

My work has taken me to the four corners of the globe, through extremes of temperature where others including myself have wilted under a blazing sun and shivered miserably in severe cold. But the Queen seems to have an untouchable serenity and self-discipline which enables her to accept any situation without fuss or visible sign of discomfort – a quality we photographers respect and would give much to share.

To be the focal point of every eye and every camera wherever you go can never be easy, yet the Queen radiates a warmth, sincerity and ease which can only spring from a natural understanding of people. When walking or talking with her, or taking what one hopes will be one's best-ever photograph, one is suddenly aware that one is relaxing, responding to her encouragement, actually enjoying the occasion. The Queen has a fantastic memory and the most charming courtesy. I have seen her concern for a colleague of mine who was taken ill and had to be flown back to England, and have experienced it myself when I once collapsed from heat-stroke. When the Queen saw me a few days later, she came over to ask me if all was now well again. I think it is this ready concern for people that endears her to them and calls forth the sturdiest loyalty from often unexpected quarters.

As a photographer I think I am extremely fortunate to have a Queen on the throne. A woman is much easier to photograph than a man and far more rewarding. People are interested in her clothes, the colours she wears, her hair-styles and jewellery, and Elizabeth II has a beautiful skin, expressive eyes and a marvellous smile. Over the years looking through the lenses of my cameras I have come to recognise her expression and moods. I try to capture her true self, to show millions of people what our Queen is really like, her kindness, her love of animals and that infectious laugh which can banish the most irritating of problems.

She did not choose to be Queen. Fate chose her, and for once in her capricious fashion, Fate has chosen well. We are indeed fortunate to have Elizabeth.

1. A Reign Begins

Treetops Hotel, perched uneasily on stilts above the scrub of the Aberdare Mountains, is perhaps the most famous centre in the world for the observation of wild birds and animals. Its fame is not unjustified on its own merits; few places are better for watching rhino, buffalo or even the elusive bongo. But it is not for buffalo or bongo that Treetops is above all remembered; it is because it was in February 1952, at the neighbouring lodge of Sayana, that a young woman of 25 went to sleep as Princess Elizabeth and woke to learn that she was Queen of England.

The Princess had left London with her husband, Prince Philip, Duke of Edinburgh, just under a week before. Her father King George VI had been forced through ill-health to cancel a projected visit to Australia and New Zealand and had asked her and her husband to stand in for him. She must have suspected that he had not long to live but he had seemed well when he waved her goodbye at London Airport. Indeed he had enjoyed several hours shooting only the day before he died. Princess Elizabeth could reasonably look forward to a few years at least as heir to the throne; in the limelight, certainly, but free from the crushing responsibilities and commitments of the crown, free to share her life with her husband and to bring up her children. Now, at the age of 25, her youth was abruptly over.

And what was it all about? The new Queen was a woman of intelligence, no intellectual but well versed in history

Treetops Hotel in the Aberdare Mountains of Kenya.

and pre-occupied by the state of her country and the world. She knew as well as anyone how dramatically things had changed during her father's reign and how much more they were likely to change while she was on the throne. What would her own role be amid this turmoil? Bagehot's celebrated statement of the rights of the constitutional monarch – to be consulted, to encourage, to warn – must have been drummed into her in the schoolroom, but what would it really mean? Would the elderly politicians who ran Britain be interested in the warnings of a young and untried woman, would they spare the time to consult her? Her father had come to terms with a socialist government, had won his ministers' respect and confidence, but when the left wing again came to power as it surely would in time, could she hope to meet with the same reception? There were plenty of people who believed and affirmed loudly that the monarchy was an expensive and futile anachronism, to be curbed or, better still, abolished altogether.

Would their view prevail? Was there a place for the monarchy in the second half of the twentieth century? It would have been extraordinary indeed if thoughts such as these had not thronged through the mind of the young Queen as she sat in the aircraft which was taking her back to a February London, back to her family, back to the sombre group of ministers, Winston Churchill at their head, who gathered to welcome Queen Elizabeth II when she returned to mount the throne.

The royal family is above all linked in the public mind with ritual and pageantry. For every once that the Queen appears in spectacular robes or gilded coach she will be seen a hundred times in hat and skirt, stepping from a motor car. And yet it is the fairy-tale Queen, the Queen of the great occasion, who captures the imagination of her people and symbolizes the monarch in the eyes of the world. No such occasion, for grandeur or significance, can approach the Coronation. This is not merely the most splendid and the most sumptuous of ceremonies, it is a solemn sacrament in which the Queen pledges herself to serve her people and receives their loyalty in return. It is what monarchy, ancient or modern, is all about. To the many millions who viewed the rite on television, what they half expected to find more or less meaningless mumbojumbo made tolerable by the glamour with which it was presented became suddenly alive and meaningful. There were plenty of cynics to declare before the event that it was indecent to waste so much money when people in the world were starving, that the whole affair would prove a colossal bore and would rebound disastrously on those who organized it. As the weeks passed and June 2, 1953 drew nearer, the criticism dwindled; when the day came it died, drowned in the uproar of a nation's acclamation.

It was not just a London affair. Every village throughout the country set up a committee to debate the pros and cons of the planting of a commemorative tree or the flood-lighting of a church; every Woman's Institute and pack of scouts organized its individual contribution. As if some hitherto undiscovered epidemic had laid the country low, every street, every house almost, broke forth into a frenzy of flags and bunting. But it was in London, of course, that it was all to happen and in London that the task of organizing the massive operation was put in hand. D-Day itself can hardly have posed more intricate or more delicate problems to those responsible.

Bernard Marmaduke Fitzalan Howard, 16th Duke of Norfolk, Earl Marshal, Hereditary Marshal and Chief Butler of England, was in overall charge of the arrangements. Nothing could better have indicated that this was a ceremony in which *all* the Queen's subjects were involved than the trick of circumstances which made a Roman Catholic responsible for organizing this supreme Protestant sacrament, the coronation of the Head of the Church of England. Nor could the contrast between his sonorous medieval titles and the business-like efficiency with which he went about his work have caught more effectively the spirit of royalty today. He carried out his daunting task with vision and flawless efficiency. (Three months before the ceremony he announced that the Queen would be crowned at approximately 12.34. The crown was placed on her head at 12.33 and 30 seconds.) The traditions of many centuries were there to guide him but countless modifications were necessary because of new needs and new possibilities. Even the Coronation Oath had to be amended to take account of developments within the Commonwealth, and the position allotted to Prince Philip during the ceremony was the subject of much debate. The role of consort to a Queen can never be easy or clearly defined; even though the phraseology rings strange today the Queen's problem was the same as that which her predecessor, Queen Victoria, had faced more than a century before – in Lord Melbourne's words, to reconcile 'the

The glittering coronation coach carrying the Queen to her crowning at Westminster Abbey on 2nd June 1953.

authority of a sovereign with the duty of a wife'. The existence of the problem and the solution to it were both made manifest when Prince Philip was the first of her subjects to kneel in homage before his Queen, but knelt beside her in the Sacrament of Communion.

There seemed no end to the details that had to be attended to, the curious crafts that were harnessed to the needs of the occasion. Skilled artists set about repairing the gold Coronation Coach – the Coach of State – to be drawn by eight greys and weighing four tons. The panels painted by Cipriani for George III were cracked, the upholstery worn and the wheels in need of resetting. The Coronation Chair, made to the order of Edward I to contain the Stone of Scone which had been captured from the Scots in 1296, was meticulously overhauled. Completed in 1301 at the cost of one hundred shillings, it had been used at every coronation since that of Edward II in 1308, and so was not unnaturally in need of a little attention.

To accommodate the multitudes who would flow into London for June and to provide them with a view of the proceedings was a gargantuan undertaking. Tiered seating for 7000 people was built in Westminster Abbey itself; so strict was the security that, every evening, sixty bunches of keys were handed over to the authorities. The route of the procession was set with stands able to seat 110,000 people while a further 500,000 were to camp by the side of the streets. Along the Thames Embankment, 2·6 square feet were allocated to every child to sit or stand in. A quarter of a million Americans paid two guineas for a seat among the chimney pots or up to fifty guineas for ground floor accommodation. Forty-four thousand bus trips on sixty-five key routes were scheduled to run in and out of London. Newspapers advised their readers not to wear hats or carry umbrellas; to wear low heels, carry packed lunches and bring barley sugar for the children.

Elizabeth in 1952 became Head of the Commonwealth, Queen of Australia, Canada, New Zealand, South Africa,

A simple white gown offsets the splendour of the Queen's blue and crimson mantle and insignia of the Order of St Michael and St George, founded in 1818

Westminster Abbey is the scene of much royal activity besides the Coronation. Here, carrying the traditional posy, the Queen leaves Westminster Abbey after the Maundy Service. One man and one woman for every year of her age receive the Royal Maundy annually – a gift of specially minted silver coins replacing the food and clothing distributed in the days of Charles II.

Pakistan, Ceylon and a plethora of colonies, protectorates and dependent territories of varying constitutional status. Since then there have been important changes, the list has shrunk significantly, but the importance of the Commonwealth and her role within it has always been to the fore in the Queen's life and mind. Nowhere was this more marked than at the Coronation. Rulers and representatives poured in from every country: four Tanganyikan Chiefs in full tribal dress and crimson tarbooshes, 32 Canadian boy scouts with the same scout colour packed in their cases as had been used at the coronations of 1911 and 1937. During the ceremony the Queen wore a pair of gold armills, or bracelets, which are traditionally royal emblems but had probably not been used at a coronation since that of King Edward VI in 1547. They were a special gift from Members of the Commonwealth and thus symbolized at the heart of this antique rite the presence of people and countries unimaginable when last they had been used.

To supplement still rationed foods, everyone was allocated an extra pound of sugar and four ounces of margarine; while manufacturers received additional allowances of sugar and fat for potato crisps, toffee apples, popcorn and candyfloss. Even without such bounty, however, the people of London were in a mood to celebrate. Not even an unseasonably cold and wet night could depress them. All along the route at dawn on coronation day campers stretched cramped, damp limbs. Hot tea and coffee, sausages and sandwiches, worked wonders, and spirits zoomed. Between 4.30 and 8.30 a.m. buses were arriving in central London at the rate of a thousand an hour and people were pouring into the capital from the home counties and beyond. One London firm baked three thousand five hundred extra loaves and, in two hours, four thousand breakfasts were served at the House of Commons.

While excitement mounted in the streets, haversack rations for the thirty thousand soldiers taking part were being issued: 1 cheese roll, 1 meat roll, 1 bar milk chocolate,

1 slice fruit cake, 1 apple, 2 ozs barley sugar. This, it was officially estimated, would keep them safely on their feet. Coronation soldiers throughout the ages must have been issued with similar rations, for since the Norman Conquest our kings and queens have been crowned at Westminster and soldiers have always played their part.

It is strange, looking back, to remember that there were officials who wanted to ban television cameras from the Abbey. The Queen herself wished the ceremony to be televised and, because of this, twenty million people throughout Britain and five million across the Channel were able to share it with her. From the moment she stepped into her coach at Buckingham Palace, through the long processions to and from the Abbey and the Coronation itself, television cameras faithfully and perfectly recorded a page of history.

The Queen entered the Abbey wearing the crimson velvet Parliamentary Robe and a solemn procession conducted her up the nave to the sanctuary, led by Abbey clergymen, the Archbishops of Canterbury and York and officers of state carrying the regalia. This included the great two-handed Sword of State, a large broadsword made for Charles II in 1689, and the Swords of Justice and Mercy. Three bishops followed, then came the Queen, on either side of her the Bishop of Durham and the Bishop of Bath and Wells. Six Maids of Honour carried her train, a bodyguard of Gentlemen-at-Arms accompanied her and finally, after members of the Household, came the Yeomen of the Guard. As the Queen drew level with the choir, the Scholars of Westminster School greeted her with their traditional cry '*Vivat Regina Elizabetha, vivat, vivat*'. In the sanctuary the Queen knelt for a few moments in prayer, then moved to her Chair of State. The Coronation Ceremony began.

First came the Queen's presentation and acceptance by acclamation. The Oath followed, in which she swore to govern her peoples according to their respective laws and

Head of the Church of England but Queen of all her subjects of whatever creed, the Queen in 1961 pays a state visit to His Holiness Pope John. It was her second visit to the Vatican. Her first was before her accession in 1951 for a private audience with Pope Pius XII.

Relaxed and happy at a ball at Valetta Palace, Malta 1967.

OPPOSITE
Three generations: Princess Anne wearing the sash of the Order of the House of Orange, with her grandmother and mother both wearing the sash of the Grand Cross of the Order of the Netherlands Lion, at Windsor during the State visit of Queen Juliana and Prince Bernhard in 1972.

1972 with the Duchess of Windsor at the entrance to the Windsors' home in the Bois de Boulogne, Paris. The Duke had planned to be present but was too ill to join his guests.

customs and to preserve their true religion. Then, with the Queen seated in the Chair of State, the Archbishop of Canterbury began the service of the Holy Communion, continuing until he reached the Creed. During the singing of an anthem the Queen was divested of her crimson robe and left the Chair of State for the Coronation Chair – King Edward's Chair. Holy oil from the Ampulla was poured into the Anointing Spoon, believed to have been used in 1199, and the Archbishop touched the Queen with it on her hands, breast and head. The most mystical and sacred part of the Service, it represented divine confirmation of the people's choice and was first recorded in 785. It is this anointing that gives the Sovereign claim to the royal title.

There followed the Queen's investment with the white *Colobium Sindonis*, a simple austere garment in which she looked defenceless and very young. Over this was placed the Close Pall, a sleeved robe of cloth of gold lined with crimson silk, and the sword belt. The Golden Spurs signifying chivalry were brought to the Queen; she touched them and they were returned to the altar. Then the Archbishop took the Jewelled State Sword set with emeralds, diamonds and rubies, the Sovereign's personal sword and the most beautiful of the five Swords of State, and, accompanied by the bishops, placed it in the Queen's hands. She returned it, showing she placed her sword at the service of the Church, and it was set again upon the altar.

So the ancient forms were carried out until there arrived the supreme moment when the Archbishop, having first set St Edward's Crown on the altar, held it high above the Queen, lowering it slowly to place it upon her head. As he did so the people cried 'with loud and repeated shouts':

Another sort of procession, though little less stirring than that at her own Coronation. An unforgettable six-mile drive to Mexico City in 1975, culminated in the most fantastic tickertape reception I have ever seen.

God save the Queen! Immediately princes and princesses, peers and peeresses and the Kings of Arms put on their coronets. The sixteen silver State Trumpets sounded forth and some eighty feet above the high altar from a gallery crammed with engineers, radio and television equipment, the signal flashed out: 'The Queen is crowned!' Faraway the great guns of the Tower of London boomed their own salute.

Anointed and crowned, the Queen received the Archbishop's blessing. Leaving St Edward's Chair, she moved to the raised throne facing the altar and was 'lifted into it by the Archbishop and Bishops and other Peers and solemnly inthronised or placed therein'. At that historic moment, Elizabeth II took possession of her kingdom. She received the homage of princes and peers, then the service of the Holy Communion was resumed. The Queen set aside the crown until after the final benediction, when she descended from the throne and retired to St Edward's Chapel. Here she was arrayed in sovereign splendour to meet her people, and exchanged the heavy St Edward's Crown for the lighter, more comfortable, Imperial State Crown. A most magnificent symbol of earthly rule, it is set with three thousand and ninety-three jewels including the great ruby given to the Black Prince in the fourteenth century; the second Star of Africa – part of the fabulous Cullinan diamond – and a sapphire said to have come from the ring of Edward the Confessor.

Minutes later, when the Queen appeared at the great West door of the Abbey, the Sceptre with the Cross in her right hand, the Orb in her left, the crowds seemed for a moment transfixed. Then a roar of welcome rose up from the massed thousands awaiting her. It was picked up and carried in a tidal wave of sound on, on and away into the distance, down Whitehall and far beyond. The great procession through the heart of her capital was still to come, the festivities had hardly begun, but in its truest sense the Coronation was over. Elizabeth was Queen and had stepped out to join her subjects. The memory would fade over the next 25 years, the glamour and the glory pass away to be replaced by the crises and frustrations of everyday existence, but at that moment nothing else seemed to matter. It was the supreme moment of Elizabeth, Our Queen. It remained to face the future, and to prove that there was still a place for monarchy in the post-war world.

2. The Corridors of Power

It was Napoleon Bonaparte – a self-made Emperor but none the less good a judge for that – who remarked that to be royal was like playing a part at the theatre and that no monarch was ever off the stage. To act successfully calls not only for talent but also for training and experience. What should have been the most important period of Queen Elizabeth's education had been denied her by her father's sudden death. Furthermore her youth had been spent in the comforting knowledge that the danger of her succeeding to the throne was no more than remote. As the daughter of a younger son there was no reason to expect that she would have to play a role more important than that of any other princess of the blood royal. Even when her uncle's abdication forced her father unwillingly on to the throne as King George VI it was still conceivable that a son might supplant her in the succession. Not until she was in the early twenties, within a year or two of the succession, could such a possibility finally be ruled out.

Her childhood had been as happy and secure as love and wisdom could make it. Playing hopscotch with her father who was difficult to beat; taking lessons with her sister, Princess Margaret; educational visits with her grandmother, Queen Mary; or holidaying in Scotland: her early years were full of all the small happenings that make up a contented childhood. When her father became King and Buckingham Palace home, life was a little more formal but there were always Windsor weekends at Royal

ntertaining that most fluential of monarchs, the hah of Iran.

*VERLEAF
he Queen of New Zealand
esides over the State
pening of Parliament in
'ellington in 1970.*

In Malta with the Archbishop and other eminent churchmen.

Lodge to look forward to, with picnics and working parties when everyone was roped in to top up the giant bonfires supervised by a garden-loving King.

With war came the mass evacuation of children from our towns and cities. For the Queen there was no question of sending the Princesses overseas. 'The children,' she said when questioned about their safety, 'will not leave unless I do; I shall not leave unless their father does; and the King will not leave the country in any circumstances whatever.' So the children went to Windsor with officers of the Grenadier Guards joining them for household meals.

In 1942 Princess Elizabeth was appointed Colonel of the Grenadier Guards and on her sixteenth birthday carried out her first public engagement – inspecting the Regiment. She had long wanted to join the services and in 1945 was gazetted a Second Subaltern in the ATS. She took a course at the Mechanical Transport Training Centre, passed out a fully qualified driver, and by the end of the war was a Junior Commander.

Peace brought many changes. Princess Elizabeth, now twenty, began to discuss state affairs with the King and to accompany the Queen on official occasions. She was given her personal flag and coat-of-arms, a secretary and Lady-in-Waiting, and a suite of her own at the Palace. A young naval lieutenant earning all of eleven pounds a week became a frequent visitor and soon after the family returned from their South African tour in 1947, the engagement of Princess Elizabeth to Lieutenant Philip Mountbatten was announced. Their marriage service in Westminster Abbey on November 20th was followed by a message issued later that day when 'Elizabeth and Philip' thanked their fellow countrymen and well-wishers in all parts of the world 'for the loving reception given us on our wedding day . . . and the unforgettable send-off in our married life'. They were two young people who had come through the war and were looking to the future as were so many others. A year later Prince Charles was born and in the summer of 1950 with the arrival of Princess Anne, two royal prams appeared in the Park. And then, on the 6th of February, 1952, came her father's death. 'I cannot lead you in battle,' said the new Queen in her speech of accession, 'but I can give you my heart.'

To say that the Queen does not exercise absolute power, that her court is not the centre of executive authority, is to state the obvious. Indeed, even in the palmiest days of monarchy, the Kings and Queens of Great Britain tended to stop well short of the autocratic. Theoretically, of course, the Queen's powers are still enormous. As fount of justice and of honours; Head of the Church, the Armed Forces, and the Commonwealth; the Privy Council her instrument; her consent essential for the passage of all legislation – she could, it would seem, bring the country to a standstill or impose her will upon her subjects. That she does not wish to, and could not if she did; that she can operate only through her ministers and parliament; is a fact so much emphasised that it is sometimes forgotten how much the Queen has to do and how massive a bureaucracy is needed to make her work possible.

If the Queen is to do her job properly, if she is indeed 'to be consulted and to have the right to advise'; then she must be informed. To keep her informed on every aspect of national and international affairs calls for an efficient and powerful machine; able to keep in touch with every department in London and every agency of government throughout the Commonwealth. Still more, if she is to carry out the formal duties of Head of State a formidably efficient and expensive organization must sustain her. Her public appearances represent the merest tip of an iceberg of planning and preparation, the price both Queen and country pay for having a symbol of leadership more magnificent and in many ways more practical than that enjoyed by any republican state. The casual visitor inspecting the bleak and uncompromising facade of Buckingham Palace may reasonably wonder how one medium-sized family, with only two children still at school, can need so cumbersome a home. They forget that the Palace is a hotel for the very grandest guests, a suite of reception rooms for the most splendid of public gatherings, an office block from which the business of monarchy is transacted – and only last, sometimes a bad last, a family home.

It is characteristic of the rather muddled sense of history

During the traditional Edinburgh season the Queen, at a Holyroodhous. garden party, shelters from an almost equally tradition. Edinburgh shower.

With that most eminent of
Commonwealth elder
statesmen, Robert Menzie
then Prime Minister of
Australia, who was
knighted by the Queen in
Canberra in 1963.

RIGHT
Queen Juliana and Prince
Bernhard of the Netherla
on a State visit in 1972
with the Queen and Princ
Philip at Windsor.

which pervades the British Isles that though many of the people who keep the machine of monarchy in motion bear titles which date back to the Middle Ages, few of them are actually doing work which would seem familiar to their predecessors. An exception is the most magnificent of them all, the Lord Great Chamberlain, who is still concerned with matters of state ceremony. The Office of Lord Great Chamberlain dates back to Henry I. Once head of the sovereign's personal household and all royal palaces, he is now responsible for arrangements when the sovereign attends Parliament and is an important officer of state at coronations. He stands on the left of the sovereign in Westminster Abbey, fastens the clasp of the Imperial Mantle after investiture and puts on the purple robes before the procession leaves the Abbey. He also makes arrangements for the lying-in-state of the dead monarch at Westminster Hall.

The Senior Officer of the Household is the Lord Chamberlain. Originally a deputy of the Lord Great Chamberlain, he long ago acquired his independence, taking over all ceremonial duties to do with the household and carrying a white staff. He also wears a gold key, symbol of his office. He is in charge of court ceremonial, arrangements for weddings, garden parties and visiting Heads of State, and for communication with Commonwealth countries on ceremonial matters. Carrying out the Queen's wishes, he appoints royal chaplains, physicians and surgeons, superintends the royal art collection and administers some of the residences.

For centuries the Lord Steward was responsible for management of the Palace-below-Stairs. This included catering for state banquets and all royal entertaining; the appointment and supervision of staff, and payment of all household expenses. Although he still retains the titular authority and on ceremonial occasions, like the Lord Chamberlain, bears a white staff as emblem of his position, these duties are now borne by the department of the

Another Scottish occasion. The Queen and Prince Philip arrive at St Giles' Cathedral, Edinburgh, wearing the plumed hat, mantle and insignia of the Order of the Thistle, second only in seniority to the Garter.

Master of the Household. The Treasurer and Comptroller are political appointments, changing with a change of government, and the Coroner of the Household exercises jurisdiction in all the royal palaces and wherever the sovereign may be staying.

The Treasurer of the Household, indeed, is a perfectly ordinary member of parliament whose real role is that of Government Whip in the House of Commons. So too is the Comptroller and the Vice-Chamberlain, who adds to his duties as Whip the responsibility, whenever parliament is sitting, of sending the Queen each day a confidential report on what has been going on. Nor do the Captains of the Gentleman-at-Arms and Yeomen of the Guard have functions as picturesque as their titles suggest; together with three other Lords-in-Waiting they act as Whips in the House of Lords. They are, in fact, professional politicians masquerading as courtiers. The Lord Chamberlain, Lord Steward, Master of the Horse and non-political Lords-in-Waiting on the other hand are appointed by the Queen, though they are bound never to vote against the Government of the day.

The Queen may also if she wishes, call upon the services of the Clerk of the Closet, a bishop whose duty used to be to 'attend at the right hand of the Sovereign in the Royal Closet during Divine Service to resolve such doubts as may arise concerning spiritual matters'. Her Mistress of the Robes is a person of high rank, seldom below that of a duchess, who is in attendance on all state occasions. She is also responsible for the duties of the Ladies-in-Waiting who are on duty in rotation, attending the Queen when she goes out and dealing with her personal correspondence.

There is always an equerry in waiting upon the sovereign; an officer of the armed services, drawn in turn from the Navy, Army and Air Force and serving for three years. The Treasurer to the Queen and Keeper of the Privy Purse deal with all financial matters; the Privy Purse Office being responsible for all the Queen's private and personal financial affairs, private estates, etc., while the Treasurer looks after official matters and the Civil List, including wages and the costs of the monarchy. One of the favourite entertainments of the popular press is estimating the private fortune of the Queen; guesses varying from a mere £2 or £3 million to £50–£60 million according to the taste of the authority. Her possessions – in pictures, jewellery, houses and the like – are of course of fabulous value, but since it is out of the question that they should ever be sold, their value can reasonably be ignored in any calculations. All that can be said with confidence is that the Queen is a very rich woman, that her commitments are also enormous and that maintaining the monarchy on anything like its present scale is an expensive business both for the Queen and country. Whether it is worth the cost is a question everyone must decide for themselves; it is perhaps significant that every public opinion poll of any statistical value shows that support for a republic, always small, diminishes every year.

At the heart of the web of power sits the Private Secretary: a mundane title compared with that of Captain of the Yeomen of the Guard but the repository of vast influence both inside and outside the Palace. The Private Secretaries are usually chosen personally by each sovereign. The post lapsed in 1688 but was revived by George III in 1805. At the beginning of Queen Victoria's reign Lord Melbourne more or less doubled the roles of Prime Minister and Private Secretary and Prince Albert took over the duties after Melbourne's fall. After the Prince's death the post was once more revived. Most of the work with which the Queen deals is channelled through his office, he provides the link between her and her governments at home and in the monarchical Commonwealth countries and is responsible for her official programme and all correspondence. It was George III again who, because he felt so many lies were being told about him, appointed the first Court Newsman at a salary of £45 a year, forerunner of today's busy Press Office.

The royal love of the race is particularly cared for at one meeting – Royal Ascot in June. Her Majesty's Representative supervises, amongst other duties, the distribution of vouchers for the royal enclosure. Queen Anne founded Ascot race-course, initiating the traditional State drive to the course which takes place each day of the meeting in June.

In state processions the Master of the Horse rides immediately behind the Queen. Once a considerable power in the land, he now has titular charge of the Queen's stables but the Crown Equerry is responsible for the Royal Mews, housing horses, carriages and, less romantically, the cars required for the family's daily needs.

Most exotic of all those attached to the royal household are the thirteen members of the Corporation of the College of Arms in England and Wales. There are three Kings of Arms: Garter, Clarenceux and Norroy and Ulster. Garter is both King of Arms of the Most Noble Order of the Garter and Principal King of Arms, and is responsible to the Earl Marshal for the conduct of the ceremonial introduction of peers into the House of Lords. There are six Heralds: Windsor, Chester, Lancaster, York, Richmond and Somerset, and the four Pursuivants carry the splendid titles of Rouge Croix, Bluemantle, Rouge Dragon and Portcullis. As well as researching, verifying and recording arms and genealogies, they attend upon the sovereign on great occasions and make proclamations.

This almost overpowering burden of history, coupled as it is with the realities of an active and highly mechanized living institution, can induce feelings of incredulity. Not every family after all, can produce in the same household a Rouge Dragon and corgis called Honey, Bee, Heather and Buzz. What other individual has Ancient Rights to treasure trove, wrecks, mute swans and sturgeon caught in the sea below London Bridge?; historical delights to set beside the computers and helicopters of the monarchy's day to day operations. The royal household is a museum, but a

With another man of power, this time President Pompidou at the Elysée Palace.

museum almost miraculously meeting the demands of contemporary society. There are people who say that it is doing the wrong job but few indeed who deny that what it *does* do it does with remarkable efficiency.

3. The Glitter and the Gold

It is one of our more illogical requirements of royalty that they must be human but they must also be grand. We need to know they can be happy and sad and make mistakes as we can, understanding if not sharing on the same level the hard economics of home budgeting, but perversely we also require them to have occasional moments of glory, to raise us above the humdrum of every day and remind us as no one else can of the pageantry and glory of our heritage. As a royal photographer, I know that no monarchy in the world evokes a sense of history more brilliantly than our own. No matter what mutterings about the expense, waste of time or living in the past precede such great occasions, in the end we look, listen and smugly acknowledge that no one else could put on a show like it. And no one could.

Amongst her many titles the Queen is head of the Army, Navy and Air Force and accordingly they owe allegiance to her and not to the government. If her interest lies more deeply in any one service, it could be the Army. Her knowledge of military history is immense and she is an expert on uniform, so it seems particularly fitting that every June she celebrates her official birthday, which is also Commonwealth Day, by Trooping the Colour. Long ago when battles were fought on the field, the Colour was a rallying point and trooped regularly at the end of a day's march to give every soldier an opportunity to identify it at close quarters. It was then escorted to its lodging place for the night and returned to the Battalion next morning. Now

Glitter and Gold, oriental style. A state banquet in the Grand Palace at Bangkok. The Queen stands between King Bhumibol and Queen Sirikit.

OPPOSITE
A night at the opera – a grand and very royal occasion at the Royal Opera House, Brussels. With the Queen and Prince Philip are King Baudouin and Queen Fabiola of Belgium, her brother-in-law Prince Albert, Prince of Liege, and his lovely wife Princess Paola.

each year the five regiments of Foot-Guards by turn troop their Colour before the Queen who is Colonel-in-Chief of all regiments of the Household Division. They still receive extra pay for the occasion – 65p for sergeants, 15 for guardsmen.

From Buckingham Palace Her Majesty, riding side-saddle and wearing the uniform of the regiment whose colour is to be trooped, is escorted down the Mall to Horse Guards Parade by the glittering Household Cavalry. This is a collective title given to the two senior regiments of the Army: the Life Guards, originally commissioned from royalists by Charles II in Holland before his restoration, and the Blues and Royals. The massed mounted bands, Standard Bearer and four divisions of the Sovereign's Escort have formed up in front of the Guards' Memorial and other members of the royal family arriving in open

Spectacular in her scarlet robe, the Queen descends the steps of St Paul's Cathedral following a service of thanksgiving for the Order of the British Empire.

carriages have preceded the Queen.

On the stroke of eleven she enters the parade ground and as she arrives at the saluting base receives a royal salute. The last notes of the national anthem fade and she moves away to ride slowly through the ranks of her Household Division. Finishing her inspection, she wheels to face the great assembly before her. Now begins the serious business of the Trooping, a magnificent spectacle of military precision, of marching and counter-marching, brilliant colour and music from the massed bands to raise the roofs of half Whitehall. The hour-long operation completed, the Queen at the head of her troops rides back to the Palace.

On a more modest scale but no less flamboyant and historically still more enthralling is the meeting of the Most Noble Order of the Garter. There are many stories as to how this Order came into being, but one seems particularly pertinent. At the Battle of Crecy, Edward III took the garter from his leg and, holding it aloft, showed it to his soldiers as an unbroken circle, an emblem to which every-one could rally. Perhaps at that moment he conceived the idea of an order of chivalry whose knights should band together and, faithful to God, relieve poverty, curb the vulgar spending of the rich and be ready to give their lives to save others. It was a brave vision and, through the King, translated into fact. In 1348 he appointed his son, the Black Prince, and twenty-four young heroes of the French wars, to be founder knights of his Order.

For more than five hundred years, St George's Chapel, Windsor, has been the home of this, the world's oldest order of chivalry. One of the most beautiful in Europe, the Chapel was built in several stages: the choir and the aisles were finished and roofed between 1477 and 1483; the nave, started the latter year, was roofed in wood and lead in 1496; while the magnificent stone vaulting was completed in 1528. By continually experimenting over three centuries, successions of builders succeeded in transferring pro-gressively more of the great weight of the roof from the

Windsor, and in brilliant sunshine the Queen and Prince Philip walk in procession to St George's Chapel for the annual service of thanksgiving for the oldest and most noble order of chivalry in the world, the Order of the Garter.

walls to the buttresses. This made it possible to convert the walls into an almost continuous area of glass, broken only by slender shafts of stone. Stand and look at this miracle of construction and it appears as delicate and fragile as lace, a glorious tribute to skill, patience and sheer hard work. The great west window with its jewel-like setting of stained glass, was painstakingly taken to pieces in the last war and, not for the first time in history, hidden away for safety.

In the choir the wooden stalls are heavily carved with animals and figures, some telling the legend of St George, others the story of the Gospel. Some are satirical, others simply decorative. The stall of every Knight of the Garter since its foundation bears his name on a brass plate; above hangs a banner bearing his coat of arms, the colours glowing softly in the shadows. On the canopy is a helmet surmounted by his crest and at the back of the stalls hang the enamelled shields each with its coat of arms, the earliest dating from the fourteenth century. There is no assembly of heraldic enamel to equal it in the world.

To St George's every year the Queen and her Companions of the Order come to their service. It is a curiously personal occasion for the Queen, much of it taking place in her own home. On the Monday of Ascot week Her Majesty holds a chapter or meeting of the Knights at Windsor Castle when new Knights are invested. In the morning a Knight Elect receives the insignia from the Queen's hands. As sovereigns have done for six centuries before her, she buckles the blue and gold garter to his left leg, places the blue Riband over his left shoulder, affixes the Star and invests him with the blue Mantle and Collar of gold.

After luncheon, Knights new and old leave in procession for St George's Chapel with Troopers of the Household Cavalry in helmets and armour and with sabres drawn, lining the royal way. At the head come the Deputy Constable and Lieutenant Governor of the Castle, and the

Part of the pageantry of London's year : the Queen with Prince Philip driving the Irish State Coach to open Parliament in 1971.

55

Military Knights of Windsor in their gay scarlet coatees and cocked hats of black and gold, followed by the Officers of arms in richly embroidered tabards. Then come the Knights of the Garter themselves, resplendent in velvet mantles of that same deep blue prescribed by Edward III over six hundred years ago, and the graceful white plumed hats – often frisked by wind to give photographers the hoped-for movement that brings their pictures alive. A sturdy detachment of the Queen's Bodyguard of the Yeomen of the Guard in long-skirted Restoration coats completes the procession. Slowly it moves up the great stone stairway into the Chapel.

A fanfare of silver trumpets heralds the Sovereign's arrival and the national anthem is played. If there are new Knights to be installed, the Queen gives notice: 'It is our pleasure that the Knights Companions be installed'. Their names are called, then Garter King of Arms and Black Rod lead them to their stalls. Their oath of chivalry has already been taken in the Throne Room of the Castle and the service that follows is brief: a psalm, the lesson, an anthem and prayer of thanksgiving for the foundations of the Order, and the final joyous Te Deum to send the echoes flying. The procession re-forms, the trumpets sound and the Sovereign leaves.

Though today some at least of the Knights of the Garter take especial pride in their *lack* of noble lineage, it remains an exceedingly exclusive body. Several times a year the Queen distributes honours on a more generous scale to all those who, for one reason or another, have been deemed to deserve well of the country and have been distinguished in the two Honours Lists published at the New Year and on the official birthday. 'The throne is the fount of honour, not a pump', warned Lord Palmerston, and there are those who consider that the system is devalued by the unduly lavish distribution of awards. Others believe, on the contrary, that still more should be given while yet others do not complain about the quantity but argue that the reci-

Inspecting Guards of Honour is a common feature of royal ritual but few inspections can have been more colourful than this one in Fiji and certainly none much hotter 105° in unhappily almost non-existent shade).

pients are badly chosen. A final group of critics claim that the whole idea of honours is ridiculous; an anachronism fit for Ruritania rather than this brave new Britain. Few of those who have actually received honours – whether senior civil servant, alderman or professional footballer – seem to see much wrong with the system. Whatever the rights or the wrongs of the matter the fact remains that the Queen does hold Investitures and that few who have been present come away untouched by the occasion. Perhaps the warmth and friendliness of the officials concerned and still more of the Queen herself, surprises them. Of course it is not easy to relax in a Palace, the fact of being there is a little overwhelming to most people. But from start to finish everything is done to simplify formalities and make the occasion a proud and happy one for everyone concerned.

Those who are to be honoured, their friends and relatives, arrive at Buckingham Palace soon after ten in the morning, walk through the porticoed Grand Entrance and climb the crimson-carpeted Grand Staircase with its gleaming marble sculptures and royal portraits, and

The Mall, London 1963, beflagged and brilliant with all the splendour of ceremonial for the State visit of King Baudouin of the Belgians.

flanked by the Queen's Bodyguard. Designed by Nash and built of Italian marble, this superb stairway leads to the State Apartments. From here guests are ushered into the Ball Room, one hundred and twenty-three feet long and sixty feet wide and lit by six immense chandeliers. At the west end is the throne dais with crimson hangings from the Delhi Durbar, and at the opposite end in the musicians' gallery a string band is playing as it does throughout the ceremony. Gentlemen-ushers help direct guests to the rows of white chairs with red satin covers and, a few minutes before eleven, five Yeomen of the Guard take their places round the throne. With various members of her household, the Queen comes through a white and gold

The British believe they manage state pageantry uniquely well but probably no other country on earth could have matched the incredible state drive to the Rashtrapati Bhavan Palace in New Delhi in 1961 when an estimated two million people crowded the route – barely half a mile long.

doorway and steps on to the dais; the Lord Chamberlain stands facing her and the national anthem is played. An equerry hands a sword to the Queen and the simple timeless ceremony begins.

The knights elect come forward in turn to kneel on a crimson stool before their sovereign, who lightly touches each with the sword, first on his right shoulder, then on his left. He stands, they shake hands, he steps back three paces, bows and moves away. Medals are handed to the Queen on a small velvet cushion. Those receiving them move slowly towards her; as each medal is affixed, she smiles and has a brief conversation before turning to the next person. The award of honours completed, the Lord Chamberlain returns to his place facing the Queen, the national anthem is again played and another investiture has taken place. It is one of hundreds down the centuries but the only one for those honoured that day.

Few people are so blasé that they would not find an invitation to penetrate the forbidding walls of Buckingham Palace a source of some excitement. For most of us the best chance lies in an invitation to one of the Queen's Garden Parties. This form of royal entertainment was introduced by Queen Victoria but she would be surprised indeed if she could see the way her innovation has evolved. Where she expected to meet, and did meet, only the top strata of society, her great-great-granddaughter is interested in people from every race and walk of life. Ninety-five per cent of the 27,000 or so guests invited each year are in public life and during the season some five hundred organizations are represented.

On three Thursday afternoons in July, soon after three o'clock, long lines of cars start moving up the Mall and guests begin arriving at the Palace, everyone hopeful that the sun will shine at least part of the time. It rarely does more. From the Bow Room they walk through the Terrace and one of the most extensive lawns in the world, to await the arrival of the Queen. There are three large marquees

Dressed for the great occasion as so many times during her year, this time in Sydney, Australia, on the Commonwealth tour in 1963 when the Queen and Prince Philip attended Canberra's fiftieth Anniversary celebrations.

providing tea and chocolate cake – one for the royal family, one for diplomats and another for the general public. About four o'clock the Queen, Prince Philip and various members of the family join their guests in the garden. If the sun does shine it is an enjoyable, peculiarly English way of passing a summer's afternoon; even if it rains the sense of occasion is still there.

But Buckingham Palace is at its most majestic for one of the state banquets held in honour of some visiting Head of State. This is the sort of occasion which tests the machinery to the full and which shows the great house at its best, playing the role for which it was designed. The Master of the Household and the Palace Steward make the arrangements, planned meticulously to the smallest detail. Guests climb the Grand Staircase, lined by the Yeomen of the Guard in ruffs and scarlet tunics. No one is announced but gentlemen-ushers direct each guest through the State Apartments to the Music Room. Decorated in ivory and gold with eighteen columns topped with gilt Corinthian capitals, it is an elegant and beautiful room lit by the finest chandeliers in the Palace. Here the guests are presented to the Queen and move through the Blue Drawing Room and East Gallery to the Ball Room where Yeomen of the Guard carrying halberds are positioned round the walls. Tables overlaid with white damask are set with gold plate, and centre-pieces of flowers compliment whenever possible the guest of honour – when the President of Germany was invited, the pink and crimson roses matched exactly the painted roses of the Meissen porcelain.

The Queen's Page stands directly behind the Queen's chair. It is an occasion for full state livery. The footmen wear scarlet coats decorated with gold braid, scarlet plush knee breeches, pink silk stockings and buckled shoes. Senior servants wear black and gold braid livery with white breeches and stockings and embroidered tunics weighing twenty-five pounds a-piece. As each course is finished, 'traffic lights' to the service corridor, amber for clearance,

Wearing a tiara of diamon and sapphires and in the mantle and insignia of the Order of St Michael and St George, the Queen arrives at St Paul's Cathedral.

...other inspection with a ...ference. Here the Queen ...spects her Yeomen of the ...uard in the grounds of ...ckingham Palace, a ...remony which takes place ...ly once every four years.

signal the page of each course to lead in his footman. Officially ninety minutes is allotted to a state banquet and at the end, pipers of the Scots Guards march round the room playing a strathspey and a reel.

The Queen rises and on the arm of her guest of honour leads the way to the State Apartments where coffee is served. The more formal part of the evening is over. Some might find it too pompous for their taste; certainly few of us would choose such surroundings for dinner seven days a week. Yet it is a uniquely splendid and rich occasion, achieving its object of making the principal guest feel that no effort is being spared to honour him. The lavish magnificence, in fact, is not extravagance for the sake of extravagance, it is display harnessed to the needs of the occasion. Whether Trooping the Colour, presiding over the Knights of the Garter, or giving some stately banquet, the Queen is on parade and all she does is part of an overall design. The glitter and the gold, in fact, is all part of the job.

4. Royal Odyssey

Time was when a royal tour overseas was heralded months in advance by the mass media. Today, we see a paragraph in the morning paper or hear an item on the news announcing that the Queen is going on her travels, and take it in our stride with the marmalade and toast. Time and space have telescoped, the extraordinary became the ordinary and the family, be it our own or that of the Commonwealth, is only a handful of hours away. Perhaps no other single factor has done more to change the face of the modern world.

Certainly no other factor can have done more to change the lives of the Queen and her family. Sometimes it must seem to her that she is almost constantly on the move; and not, as in the past, by leisurely sea-voyages with time to adjust and catch up on her background-reading but hurled from one society and climate to another, expected to appear after a few hours' uncomfortable flight band-box fresh and ready to face the rigours of a royal tour.

The Queen rightly believes that it is not good enough for the Queen of Australia or of Canada to play the part from London, she must go regularly to these countries and get to know her Australian and Canadian subjects. From time to time it is suggested that she should have a palace in Canberra, in Ottawa, in Wellington, and spend regular periods of the year in each country. There are formidable difficulties in the way of such a course, and as the speed of communication grows greater the need seems on the

*scene characteristic of the
art of so many royal tours,
is time at Sydney airport
here the Queen and Prince
hilip flew in from New
ealand for the bicentenary
lebrations of Captain
ook's first landing in
ustralia.*

whole to diminish. Certainly few years go by without her visiting several of the Commonwealth countries. But the Commonwealth is not the world. Queen Elizabeth, as Head of State, must pay official visits to other friendly powers; visits which, it is hoped, will cement friendly relations and encourage greater trade. Ambassador Extraordinary, Chief Promoter of British Exports, these are not roles the first Elizabeth would have relished. How far Queen Elizabeth II finds them to her liking is something she keeps to herself – it is part of the job and as such something that must be done regardless of personal inclination.

Whenever the Queen is to be out of the country for more than a few days, she has to appoint Counsellors of State to take over certain of her functions. The Counsellors – who may not dissolve Parliament or create peers in her

Britannia floodlit in Sydney Harbour alongside one of the world's most famous bridges.

absence – are appointed from Prince Philip, the Queen Mother and the four adult members of the family next in succession to the throne. In practice they are usually the Queen Mother and Princess Anne.

The first time such an occasion arose for the Queen was in her Coronation year when she and Prince Philip were away from November until the following May. Bermuda, Jamaica, Fiji, Tonga, New Zealand, Australia, Ceylon, Uganda, Malta and Gibraltar – a long haul by any standard but one with a particularly happy ending when Prince Charles and Princess Anne arrived in *Britannia* to join their parents at Tobruk. Since then *Britannia* has often provided a home when the family are on the high seas.

A joy to look at, she gleams with white paintwork, has a royal blue and red hull, a decorative gold band below the upper deck, buff coloured masts and funnel, the royal coat of arms on her bows and the royal cypher on her stern. Over four hundred feet long, she replaced the unseaworthy

Driving to the opening of the Nigerian Parliament in 1956, London's winter forgotten in the sun-drenched brilliance of the African scene.

Victoria and Albert – some of whose furniture, including some Hepplewhite chairs, found a new setting in *Britannia*. She is one of the favourite targets for those who complain that the royal family costs too much money, but few of those who saw her ablaze with lights, flaming like some rich jewel in Sydney harbour, will doubt that the money was well spent.

Her officers are usually appointed for two-year periods of duty and about half the ratings are permanent crew remaining for the rest of their service careers. In a sense *Britannia* is their home as well as the Queen's. All are volunteers from the Royal Navy and pay, allowances and leave are exactly the same though traditions of dress are not. Seamen wear their jumpers tucked inside their trousers which are finished at the back with a black silk bow; and on all blue uniforms ratings wear white badges instead of the customary red. As far as possible, all orders on the upper deck are executed without spoken words or commands, so apart from being a comfortable and happy ship, *Britannia* is unusually quiet.

As long ago as 1936, Edward VIII decided to provide air transport for the family's official duties, and the King's Flight came into being. Now the Queen's Flight, it is provided by the RAF, based in Oxfordshire, and comprises three passenger transport aircraft and two helicopters. Though seldom used for visits overseas, the Queen, the Queen Mother and Prince Philip can use the Flight on all occasions, and at the Queen's discretion it is available for other members of the family when travelling on duty. The Prime Minister, senior Ministers and visiting heads of state may also use it for official purposes. A far-sighted decision forty years ago, the Flight has been invaluable ever since.

In January 1956, the Queen and Prince Philip flew off into the winter night for a three-weeks' tour of Nigeria. Kaduna, the capital, a lovely sun-drenched garden city, had become one vast jamboree with banners, flowers,

At the Palace, Indian dancers, princesses in their own right, with palms touching in Eastern greeting, talk to the Queen

dancing and singing, and visiting horsemen camping under the stars. A durbar given in the Queen's honour must have amazed and delighted her. Two thousand horses took part, plumed and caparisoned in quilted cloth of gold, with riders in spangled burnooses and turbans of scarlet, jade and turquoise. There were jesters, tumblers, tambourines and pipes, and a charge of horsemen in chain mail who thundered to within yards of the royal stand to stop dead before the Queen and salute her.

A state visit to Sweden followed in June and the Queen and Prince Philip were afterwards joined by Princess Margaret and the late Duke of Gloucester to watch the Olympic equestrian events. 1957 was a crowded year with three state visits to Portugal, France and Denmark, and a tour of Canada when the Queen opened the twenty-third Parliament – the first sovereign ever to open parliament in Ottawa. They continued from Canada to America as guests of President Eisenhower and on to New York where the Queen addressed the United Nations General Assembly. Less than two years later she was to return to open the great St Lawrence Seaway, and visit Chicago.

1961 was a marathon year. In January the Queen and Prince Philip began a tour of India, Pakistan, Nepal, Iran and Turkey. In May they paid a state visit to Italy and the Vatican, and in November and December to the West coast of Africa – Ghana, Liberia, Sierra Leone and The Gambia. It must have been something of a relaxation the following year to have only a semi-private visit in May to the Netherlands for the Silver Wedding anniversary of Queen Juliana and Prince Bernhard. Members of nearly all the royal families in Europe were among the hundred and fifty guests, who were entertained at a glittering ball and a banquet in the three-hundred-year-old palace on the Dam, a sightseeing tour by bus of Amsterdam, and a tour of the canals by barge to admire the illuminations. Only the weather failed to live up to the occasion, when the Queen in white lace and fur stole queued to go aboard in drizzle and a biting wind.

OPPOSITE
India 1961, undoubtedly the most colourful and spectacular royal tour I have covered. When I took this photograph the sun was sinking, the light rapidly fading and I was momentarily stunned by the magnificence of the scene, fortunately reacting in time to take one of my favourite pictures.

OVERLEAF
In Maori country, Gisbourne, New Zealand, where I heard that haunting Haka *cry known to rugger enthusiasts everywhere.*

In 1963 came another major Commonwealth journey
for the Queen and Prince Philip, with brief stops in Canada
and Honolulu, before arriving at Fiji in a temperature of
105 degrees with fourteen thousand excited children
waiting to greet them. It was Sunday, so many of the Chiefs
arrived in white Sunday-go-to-Meeting suits instead of
their customary flower-garlanded skirts of grass and tree
bark. But it was a jubilant occasion celebrated with the
native wine, *kava*.

Four days later it was New Zealand with Parliament to
open, garden parties, civic welcomes and five shilling seats
at the races. Then away to Australia with rain and a
glistening sea of umbrellas at the airport, to start yet another round of art galleries, hospitals, more garden parties –
and from *Britannia* an all-important six-minute birthday
call to Prince Andrew. In Canberra, celebrating its 50th

anniversary, the Queen knighted the Prime Minister, Robert Menzies, and in Melbourne she was almost hit by a bunch of flowers hurled into her car. Chops and sausages cooked over an open fire were the menu at a bush picnic in the Snowy Mountains, and on the flame-coloured soil of Alice Springs three hundred steers kicked up such a welcoming dust that they and everyone else disappeared in an orange fog.

Tasmania's joy at seeing the Queen quickly overcame the embarrassment at having hurriedly to move the red carpet before royal guests could come ashore – a miscalculation in the placing of the dais in relation to *Britannia's* docking. A visit to the Olympic Pool, a drive to Mount Wellington, a royal speech bravely battling against a neighbouring fairground brass band, and it was back to mainland Australia, to Perth and to a farewell speech from the Queen, not surprisingly 'dazed and delighted' by the warmth of her welcome.

Canada was visited in 1964, and in 1965 there were two state visits, the first to Ethiopia and the Sudan, the second to Germany – an unqualified success. 'The Queen flew

OPPOSITE
1970 : Canada for the centenary celebrations of the North-West Territories and the Province of Manitoba. To get this photograph I spent a freezing night on the floor of the local unheated school house and dinner provided by friendly Eskimos consisted of sardines, cheese, and coffee in plastic school-cups. Members of the press were issued with a survival kit of one candle, a toothbrush and toothpaste, bottle of Coca Cola, compass, screwdriver and pliers for cameramen, and a photograph of a pretty girl . . .

Inspecting the Guard of Honour at Bonn airport with President Lubke.

over the Berlin Wall and captured Berlin!' declared one German paper. A retired postal worker was refused permission by the German authorities to present the Queen with his prize canary as such a gesture was considered unsuitable. The Queen heard of this, said she would be delighted to receive it, and the canary was duly despatched to Buckingham Palace and appointed to the royal nurseries. Everyone everywhere seemed determined to give the Queen a welcome she would remember. They succeeded.

And so down the years the travels continued: the Caribbean, Belgium, and back to Ottawa for Canada's 100th Anniversary of Confederation. Then came a state visit to Brazil, Chile and Senegal – the royal luggage including three tiaras and matching necklaces, two portable wardrobes filled with model clothes from Hartnell and Amies, a clutch of polo sticks and a quantity of frozen game birds for a banquet. In Brazil an official notice advised gentlemen not to kiss or embrace the Queen as she would, they were warned, openly reject this Brazilian custom. Instead they had to make do with gun salutes, tickertape welcomes and a royal overnight stay at a ranch. At the President's residence, his wife asked Prince Philip if the star worn on his white Air Marshal's uniform was given him last time he was in Brazil. 'Yes,' he replied with a dazzling smile, 'I've been polishing it ever since.' The farewell gift this time was two jaguars.

From Brazil to Chile, following a warm invitation from President Frei to his 'Good and big friend'. Here, between civic addresses, banquets, visiting schools and planting a tree, the Queen laid a wreath on the monument to the country's hero, who liberated the people from the Spanish, a gentleman with the unlikely name of Bernardo O'Higgins.

1969 was the year Princess Anne made her debut as a state visitor. In April she had been presented with the family Order – a miniature of the Queen surrounded by baguette diamonds – and was to have accompanied her parents to Austria. Delayed by 'flu she arrived by executive

Thailand, exotic, beautiful, brilliantly colourful, with a royal family as charming as they are generous and kind. Fresh flower petals were scattered before the Queen as she walked along the quayside from Britannia, *one of the many delightful customs practiced in the highly skilled art of Thai hospitality.*

jet in time to down her first glass of schnapps and visit the Spanish riding school in Vienna to see the famous Lippizanner horses. She had the pleasure of riding a magnificent white stallion and putting him through his paces. The farewell gifts included two biscuit-coloured Hafflinger ponies for the Queen, a table cloth and a book on Salzburg for Princess Anne. Prince Charles was sent an ice pick. A jolly family holiday, one might think – until one remembers that the Royal Family were permanently on duty; working to a gruelling tight schedule; constantly having to listen to speeches with expressions of bright interest and to reply in a way that sounded spontaneous and sincere; knowing that a single yawn or frown or ill-judged joke could reverberate around the country and turn the visit into a public relations disaster. Sight-seeing in such circumstances is not so far removed from hard work.

A year later Princess Anne was again on her travels with her parents, this time to New Zealand and Australia via Fiji and Tonga. They flew out to join *Britannia* in Fiji. In Suva six chiefs, glistening with coconut oil, resplendent in leaf skirts and anklets of shells and rattling dried seed pods, came aboard to present three whales' teeth in traditional welcome. At Tonga, under a burning mid-day sun, a gargantuan feast was set before them which included thirteen hundred sucking pigs and baskets overflowing with tropical fruits. Princess Anne, neatly tucking her legs beneath her, followed the island custom of eating with her fingers. Prince Charles joined them in New Zealand, and they arrived in Australia in time for the bicentenary celebrations of Captain Cook's first visit.

In July they were back in Canada for the centenaries of the North West Territories and the Province of Manitoba. They visited the oldest Hutterite colony, a sixteenth-century religious community where radio and television are banned, and an Indian reservation at Swan River; they attended a rodeo and ate smoked Arctic char and buttered fiddleheads – a local vegetable – at Yellowknife, where

swarms of mosquitoes and blackflies joined in the general welcome. On to the Arctic Circle where the Commissioner for the North West Territories presented Princess Anne and Prince Charles with fur-trimmed parkas – donned with alacrity. Disappointingly clouds hid the midnight sun during a short visit to Tuktoyaktuk. With Prince Philip, Prince Charles flew to the Northern Archipelago to see the work on oil exploration and, keeping his hand in, piloted the plane back to base.

Next year was British Columbia's centenary, and the Queen, Prince Philip and Princess Anne returned to join in the celebrations. Home for the summer, they were away again in October for a state visit to Turkey. Spring '72 brought a six weeks' tour of south-east Asia and the Indian Ocean taking in Thailand, Singapore, Malaysia, Brunei, the Maldive Islands, Seychelles and Mauritius. In '74 it was Cook Island, New Zealand and a number of Pacific Islands; in '75 Mexico, Hong Kong and Japan. . . .

So many miles travelled, so many countries visited. It

To be serenaded is the fate (or pleasure) of many tourists to many countries but when it happens to the Queen in Mexico there are 2000 other guests and the scene is a Presidential banquet in the Grand Palace.

seems a long while since the young Princess Elizabeth stood before a microphone in Cape Town on her twenty-first birthday and said: 'I declare before you all that my whole life, whether it be long or short, shall be devoted to your service and the service of our great imperial family to which we all belong.' The miles she and her family have since journeyed carrying out that vow would put a ring around the earth several times over.

And has it all been worth while? Worth it to the Queen, for the occasional boredom and discomfort, the disruption of her life, the long separations from her family? Worth it to the nation, for the sometimes formidable expense? There is no way of striking a balance, but if some way could be found of measuring the happiness and excitement which the royal visits have brought to multitudes the world over, I have no doubt that they would be found amply justified. As to the slightly more quantifiable results – better diplomatic relations, greater exports – it is more hard to be sure. Statesmen are hard-boiled and have short memories; a sentimental speech in January will not necessarily produce an order for an atomic power station in June. But on the whole, though professional cynics would never concur, the sum of informed opinion seems to be that a royal visit does amply pay off in terms of good will. Certainly it is not for want of hard work on the part of the Queen and Prince Philip if it does not.

5. 'Tied Cottages'

When the Queen and Prince Philip returned from one of their overseas tours, they were greeted at the Palace by the Foreign Secretary. Later the Queen remarked how strange it was to be welcomed into one's own house. Prince Philip reminded her that it was not in fact their own house, more of a tied cottage that went with the job. Buckingham Palace has gone with the job since 1837.

In 1702 the Duke of Buckingham commissioned William Winde to design a new mansion looking down the avenue planted by Charles II to form the Mall. It was a handsome building in a charming setting, the garden ending in a long terrace covered with roses and jasmine. This was deliberately built low enough to give a wide view across the meadow where cattle browsed, and a 'little wilderness full of blackbirds and nightingales' shaded the south side. Some sixty years later the house was sold to the Crown for £28,000 and straightway became the home of George III and Queen Charlotte. It was from their home that Buckingham Palace evolved as we know it today.

When George IV came to the throne in 1820, there were suggestions that a grander, more suitably imposing royal residence should be built, but George was adamant. 'If the public wish to have a palace,' he told architect John Nash, 'I have no objection to build one, but I must have a *pied-à-terre* . . . and . . . I will have it at Buckingham House.' Ultimately only the shell of the original mansion was retained but when the roof was finished the King told

Nash the State rooms were so fine that he had decided he would hold his Courts there. Nash was appalled. It was all too small, he argued, it was a residence he was building, not a palace. 'You know nothing about the matter,' retorted the King, highly displeased. 'It will make an excellent palace.'

He never lived to see it completed. The eighteen-year-old Victoria was the first sovereign to live there, driving in state from Kensington just three weeks after her accession when the royal standard was raised for the first time above London's fine new Buckingham Palace.

Nash's fears that his residence was too small for a palace proved correct, but the difficulties were not insurmountable. After her marriage to Albert, Victoria expressed a wish for a consecrated chapel and the south conservatory was duly converted in 1843. Four years later the East Front was added and some of the finest fittings from George IV's Royal Pavilion at Brighton brought to enrich it. From that time the Royal Standard, signifying the Sovereign is in residence, has flown from the East Front roof. Today it is estimated that wear and tear from London's weather – the flagstaff is seventy feet high – costs the Queen approximately four pounds a week for repairs. The East Front itself, the facade which presents itself to the public, cannot be called beautiful. Some indeed would describe it as downright ugly. But it does not lack self-confidence, it knows its place. It is every inch a palace.

One more important structural addition was to be made in 1854. Sir James Pennethorne, pupil of John Nash, removed George III's armoury and octagon library and replaced it with a ball room one hundred and twenty-three feet long and sixty feet wide. A throne dais was placed at the west end and an organ and musicians' gallery at the other. Today it is used for state balls, banquets and investitures. Below were built spacious kitchens and adjoining it in the south wing a ball supper room, now also used for diplomatic receptions. The six doorways are of mirror

Glittering crystal chandelie and superb mirrors, the White Drawing Room where the Royal Family assemble to meet their gues at State banquets and ball.

The State Dining Room in Buckingham Palace with its magnificent ivory and gold ceiling, gold chandeliers and walls lined with royal portraits; Ramsay's George III : George IV in his coronation robes by Lawrence : Queen Charlotte by Ramsay : Frederick Prince of Wales by Van Loo and Kneller's Caroline of Ansbach.

glass, the walls covered with arched mirrors reaching from the floor almost to the ceiling.

When George V came to the throne in 1910, Queen Mary, great-granddaughter of Queen Charlotte, made it her self-appointed task to trace many of the original pieces of furniture designed for Buckingham House and restore them to the private rooms. It was her delight to display the royal collections of porcelain, paintings and furniture to the finest possible advantage, and it would please her to know that this delight has been handed down and finds expression today in the Queen's Gallery. When Victoria's chapel was wrecked by a German dive bomber in 1940, the site was imaginatively used to build this gallery to display paintings and works of art from the royal collections. Small and charming, it still incorporates a chapel screened from view under a balcony which was originally the royal pew, and it is open to anyone with time to spend relaxing with some of the Queen's much-loved treasures.

Today, Victoria's afternoon Drawing Rooms and the brilliant Evening Courts of Edward VII and Alexandra have been replaced by garden, luncheon and sherry parties where guests are men and women from all over the world and from every profession. Private luncheon parties are often held in the 1844 Room named from its occupation by Emperor Nicholas I of Russia when he came to London on a goodwill visit. Decorated in white and gold with amber-coloured pillars, it is to this room that ambassadors come to present to the Queen their letters of credence to the Court of St. James, and where Privy Councils are held.

Possibly the room in the Palace best known to the outside world is the Bow Room. Crimson-carpeted and decorated in ivory and gold, guests to the royal garden parties walk through its tall glass doors to the terrace and forty-five green acres of garden beyond.

James I, who imported ten thousand mulberry trees to help establish a silk industry but forgot it was the white mulberry and not the black which is favoured by silk worms, would be astonished to find one of his original trees still standing. The twenty-five acres of lawn are happily invaded by camomile which apparently crept in unobserved, was approved and is now well and truly entrenched, ensuring a green lawn however dry the summer. The lake, complete with rosy flamingos, bronze storks presented to Edward VII at the Delhi Durbar and exquisite water-lilies, has a small island at one end where the Queen and Princess Margaret used to pitch a tent and make their camp.

One of the gardens, the Arboretum, is centred round the famous Waterloo Vase, Wellington's trophy from his victory over Napoleon. It is made out of one block of Carrara marble which in Victoria's day was planted with ivy-leaved geraniums. One spring a pair of mallard ducks

from the lake decided it could be more profitably used, moved in and raised a family. It has been mallard property ever since. Overlooking the Arboretum is the Mariners' Summerhouse, so called because of the carved figures forming the main pillars – figureheads from Her Majesty's ships presented to Queen Victoria by the Admiralty. Here, as children, the Queen and Princess Margaret often struggled with French verbs in almost country quiet in a garden where roses and lilacs, camelias, delphiniums, rhododendrons and azaleas flourish amazingly in the heart of London.

Perhaps the loveliest rhododendrons and azaleas bloom in the gardens of Royal Lodge, the Queen Mother's private home tucked away in the south-east corner of Windsor Great Park. Originally a dairy farm, it was enlarged in 1813 to become a favourite residence of George IV. Of his building, only one large room remains and it was around this that George VI arranged the house as it now stands. Pink-washed to please his Queen it has almost a continental air, and the surrounding grounds became his weekend stamping ground. 'Now that,' he once said, 'really is my garden. I made it.' And he did, opening new vistas, clearing, planting, pruning and for ever planning more improvements. This was where he most loved to come for relaxation from state affairs, mercilessly inviting everyone present, gardeners and non-gardeners alike, to join him.

One rather charming tradition which he began is now quite literally rooted here. Every family wedding bouquet contains a sprig of sweet-scented myrtle from which, after the ceremony, cuttings are taken. These are rooted and eventually planted out in tubs ensuring an unbroken supply for the wedding bouquets of future generations.

The wide stone terrace where the family dined on warm summer evenings was hedged about with rosemary and lavender and in the woodland garden the beloved rhododendrons, Kurume azaleas, pyrocanthus and lilacs vied in splendour with magnolias, maples and camelias. Beneath, in a patchwork of colours spread like a Joseph's coat beneath the shrubs, were hundreds of polyanthus and everything incredibly seemed to blossom together in one glorious riot of colour and scent.

A mile and a quarter away as the crow flies, stands Windsor Castle. It is now nine centuries since William the Conqueror erected it to protect the middle reaches of the Thames and dominate the countryside for miles around. From here Richard the Lionheart rode out to the Crusades and John, his brother, went to Runnymede to sign Magna Carta in 1215. Windsor Forest once stretched at least fifteen miles westwards and twenty miles south to Guildford, and within this area all game was preserved for the king by law. Sadly the forest has shrunk but the Great Park still extends over nearly five thousand acres and is fourteen miles in circumference. It is connected with the Castle by an avenue three miles long known as the Long Walk, created by Charles II in 1685. The spectacular walls and towers of the Castle itself are in fact largely a nineteenth century creation, the fantasy of King George IV turned into reality by the genius of his favourite architect, Wyattville. Nothing could be more imposing, more majestic; and the fact that it is an extravagant fake matters remarkably little.

During the last war, the Castle was the 'house in the country' to which the Princesses were sent for safety and where they remained for five years. Peering down from the ramparts one day, Princess Margaret watched an official black car being driven swiftly into the courtyard below and gloomily guessed it might be bringing bad news. 'Boiling lead was a pretty good idea,' she remarked thoughtfully. The Castle with its towers and battlements dwarfing the buildings clustered at its feet, has always been a wonderful place for children. 'It's a very BIG castle,' Prince Edward confided to a visitor, who suggested helpfully it might be a good place for cowboys and Indians.

The family in the grounds Frogmore, a favourite residence of Queen Victor in Windsor Home Park.

Windsor Castle in the background. Princess Anne with Prince Edward at the Royal Windsor Horse Show 1971, in their French pony carriage given by Edward VII to their great-great-grandmother Queen Alexandra.

Windsor Great Park with trainer Alison Oliver.

The Prince was indignant. 'There are no cowboys here,' he said. But there are plenty of other excitements including the shirt in which Charles I was executed, the bullet from Nelson's heart, a sword that probably belonged to Bonnie Prince Charlie and Henry VIII's armour.

The State and Private Apartments are in what is known as the Upper Ward of the Castle, consisting of all buildings east of the Round Tower – from which a well descends one hundred and sixty-five feet to the level of the Thames. For eight hundred years there have been buildings where the State Apartments now stand, but the present rooms are in effect the house built in the late 1670's for Charles II. Sovereigns have always lived in this flank of the Castle because it was impregnable and windows could safely be let into the walls.

The State Apartments with magnificent ceilings painted by Verrio, contain a wealth of paintings by Raphael, Rembrandt, Rubens, Canaletto and Van Dyck; Gobelins tapestries, carvings by Grinling Gibbons; superb carpets and glittering chandeliers; sculptures, including one of Sir Winston Churchill; and the sword surrendered to Lord Louis Mountbatten on the defeat of Japan in 1945. More than one hundred thousand visitors a year wander through these beautiful rooms which are open to the public, but the privacy of the Queen's four-storey tower on the eastern side remains unbroken.

The Private Apartments are the result of a remarkable transformation of austere fortress rooms into a warm, well-equipped and pleasant home. Large enough to hold the entire family, which Sandringham no longer is, it has become the focal point at Christmas for everyone. There is a staff dance in December in the great Waterloo Chamber, where a banquet is held on the 18th June commemorating the Battle of Waterloo; there are two or three shimmering Christmas trees often chosen on site by the Queen and Prince Philip when riding in the Park; everyone attends a carol service in St. George's Chapel or one by candlelight

Windsor is as much as anything associated in the public mind with the royal love of horses. Here the Queen rides out, her family behind her.

The Castle in more formal setting. The arrival of two Queens in 1974 – Elizabeth of Great Britain, and Margarethe of Denmark on a State visit to this country.

in the tiny church in the grounds of Royal Lodge; and a grand skirl of bagpipes awakes the entire household on Christmas morning. Seldom has the old Castle echoed more to the sound of laughter and children's voices than today.

It was something of an innovation when the Queen transferred the Christmas holiday to Windsor, but the family had outgrown the rambling old house at Sandringham, part of which has now been pulled down. Those crisp walks, when a biting wind often carrying snow whipped unchecked across the open field to sting the cheeks and eyes of anyone brave enough to venture out, are remembered with varying degrees of affection. 'Dickens in a Cartier setting,' was how Edward VIII once described their Norfolk Christmases; while George VI loved every stick and stone.

There are still flower-filled borders, trees and bushes heavy with fruit in season and glasshouses lush with peaches and grapes, but the lavish houseparties of Edward VII at the turn of the century are almost forgotten. Instead, the family turns to Wood Farm on the estate for occasional weekends away from it all. Once the home of a local doctor, the old stone house has had a face-lift; floors and roofing have been renewed, old fireplaces ripped out and central heating installed. Prince Charles and Prince Richard of Gloucester, then an architectural student, plunged enthusiastically into plans for renovation and the result is a small, comfortable home at which they can entertain their friends, shoot, bird-watch or just relax in complete privacy.

But perhaps the best loved holiday home of all is Balmoral, the castle of light grey Invergeld granite built on twenty-four thousand acres bought by the Prince Consort for Victoria in 1848. The silver Dee still flows past the castle; the salmon leap from the tumbling waters; and the same woods climb the slopes of the wild hills Victoria loved to journey over, perhaps in her tartan-upholstered

Balmoral, little changed since Prince Albert bought it for Victoria in 1848, beloved by all the family for the heather hills, salmon fishing, sailing and most of all its peace.

OVERLEAF
Sandringham, the country estate in Norfolk bought by Edward VII, when he was Prince of Wales.

'dear Scottish sociable', for picnic teas with the children in the heather. Now each summer her descendants stay at Balmoral with the Queen Mother at Birkhall, ten miles away.

In the entrance hall the statue of King Malcolm III faces one of a kilted Prince Albert, and predictably there is a wealth of tartan and deerskin rugs. The comfortable drawing room has its collection of Landseer ghillies and in the dining room hangs Winterhalter's portrait of the young Victoria. Guest rooms are on the ground floor – ministers taking the service at Crathie Church on rota often stay over Saturday and Sunday – and the Queen's private secretary has a house in the grounds to himself. Work is kept to a minimum but despatch boxes follow the Queen everywhere and are one of her daily chores even at Balmoral.

A visit to the tied cottage of another monarch. With Emperor and Empress of Japan in the grounds of the Imperial Palace, Tokio.

Out-door living is the order of most days when the weather is kind. Riding, fishing, golf, walking, picnicking, sailing and cricket: everyone has their special pleasure and at Balmoral it is possible to indulge it. For those feeling lazy, the gardens one thousand feet above sea level, filled with birdsong and the sounds of the swift flowing Dee, are a glory of simple delights where phlox, fuchsias, cherry pie and roses nudge shoulders with lilies, stocks, lavender and gentians. For the energetic eager to explore the hills there are shaggy Fell and highland ponies excellent as bare-back mounts.

Four miles from the castle Prince Charles entertains friends at Gelder Shiel Lodge; at Birkhall the Queen Mother has a caravan trailer for unexpected guests and the delight of her grandchildren, and near the river is a cottage simply furnished with cretonnes and folkweaves for the pleasure of friends who like to fend for themselves.

It's a temptation to return in the late afternoon, for tea is a splendid meal, of scones and baps and bannocks and rich fruit cake. By dusk the hills are left to the curlew and the heather and in October, the roar of the stags. Wood smoke drifts blue above the castle. Inside, logs are heaped on the fires, dinner terminated by the music of seven pipers is followed by the occasional film show, reading, talk of the day's activities and tomorrow's plans.

One by one the lights go out, voices fade, the castle settles imperceptibly to sleep. Tomorrow, the day after that – what matter? At Balmoral as everyone knows, tomorrow will take care of itself.

6. The Family Firm - 1

Nobody would pretend that the Queen has an easy life but at least she knows what she is supposed to do. The role of other members of the royal family has been, and will be so long as the monarchy survives, one of peculiar difficulty and embarrassment. They are perpetually in the limelight yet rarely play a starring role; they live in considerable style and yet are not particularly rich; they are expected by the public to follow careers, and themselves probably wish to do so, yet their royal duties impede their progress and their connections make it impossible for them to behave entirely like other people. They are fair game for every gossip writer, their marital or extra-marital affairs are pried into, they are perpetually on show; yet such glory as they have comes by courtesy of the head of their family, it is hard indeed for them to become established as personalities in their own right. The degree of success which the present generation of princes and princesses has achieved in overcoming these disabilities is a tribute both to their own determination and to the wisdom of their parents.

In the past the strains of this curious, artificial existence have been particularly marked in the bad relationships between monarchs and their children. For generation after generation the eldest son in particular has tended to set up in opposition to his parents; either politically, as the future George IV espoused the Whig cause in defiance of his father's Tory predilections; or socially, as King

...lo, with Prince Philip in ...ion at Cowdray Park in ...ssex before a wrist injury ...pped play. Prince ...arles inheriting his ...her's love of the sport, ...w maintains the ...ditional interest.

LOW
...ince Philip receiving the ...phy from the Queen on ...alf of the Windsor Park ...lo team, at Smiths Lawn ...69.

Edward VII drew his friends from a circle that his mother deemed raffish and vulgar. Anyone acquainted with British history is likely to look for evidence of such rancour and rivalries in the royal family today. They will look in vain. Even the most energetic critic of the modern monarchy would hardly deny that, as a family, they are singularly united and devoted. The solidarity of their family background is perhaps the greatest single asset which the sons and daughter of Queen Elizabeth II enjoy as they launch themselves on their public lives. They will have every need of it, for only the most short-sighted and die-hard traditionalist would deny that the way ahead is going to be difficult and that much skill and courage will be called for if they are to adapt themselves to the needs of the coming decades.

That they have so far shown themselves ready and able to tackle the problems as they arise is in large part the achievement of their father. From the beginning Prince Philip was determined that his children should learn what went on beyond the Palace walls. He wanted them to realise that the rough and tumble of life constituted a large part of it, and that in order to lead and help people it must first be understood how they lived and worked. His own early life was hardly that of the story book Prince. The Kings of Greece stem from a branch of the Danish royal family, and Philip, a Mountbatten on his mother's side but Danish through his father, Prince Andrew, was in line to succeed his uncle, the Greek King Constantine. But when the Greek throne toppled, not for the first or final time, the young Philip was smuggled out of the country aboard a British battleship and eventually came to Britain.

A prep school at Cheam was followed by Gordonstoun and the Royal Navy, and in January 1940 he emerged as a midshipman in the battleship *Ramillies*. Promoted lieutenant two and a half years later, he became one of the youngest officers in the Navy to be second-in-command of a large destroyer. On the eve of his wedding to Princess Elizabeth,

George VI created him Duke of Edinburgh, Earl of Merioneth, Baron Greenwich and a Knight of the Garter, titles which heralded the life he was destined to lead. In 1950 he took over his first command as Lieutenant-Commander of HMS *Magpie*, a frigate based in Malta, but the following summer went on indefinite leave pending the proposed Commonwealth tour of the King and Queen. It was in fact the end of his active service career.

With the accession of Elizabeth II, enormous opportunities confronted him and his role became increasingly more important in the life and work of the country. Fascinated by scientific and industrial development, he plunged into a whirlwind of new activities, becoming President of the British Association for the Advancement of Science and emphatically maintaining that the nation's wealth and prosperity were governed by the application of science to its industries and commerce.

With his passion for accuracy and detail, he travelled the country, visiting research stations and laboratories, going down coal mines, inspecting factories, engineering works and industrial plants, always with the minimum of fuss and the maximum of personal viewing and interviewing. 'There will be no flags, no reception committees, no guards of honour, no formal presentations, and no red carpets,' one Chairman told his workers. 'The Duke wants to see a factory as it is every normal working day, a thing he can never do on formal occasions.' Those formal occasions were now things of the past. A visit from the Duke of Edinburgh meant a personal fact-finding mission starting on the shop floor, and if eyebrows were raised he was not concerned.

Succeeding George VI as patron of the Industrial Welfare Society, he launched in 1956 a conference at Oxford on the human problems of industrial communities within the Commonwealth – where delegates from the various Commonwealth countries represented studied in particular those factors which make for satisfaction,

In the royal train en route for Christmas at Sandringham, 1962.

OPPOSITE
The young Princess Anne, then a mere spectator, at the Royal Windsor Horse Show.

efficiency and understanding in industry and the community around it. When he became a British subject, the Duke had renounced his royal title but in 1957 the Queen granted him the style and dignity of a Prince of the United Kingdom, and in future he was to be known as HRH The Prince Philip, Duke of Edinburgh. So it was as a royal Prince that he launched a second equally successful Study Conference in Canada in 1962, a third in Australia in 1968, and a fourth, again at Oxford, in 1974.

A book two inches thick lists the organizations to which he belongs or of which he is patron, president or chairman. Godfather to twenty-five children, he years ago nailed his colours to the mast in support of youth. His Award Scheme, originally instituted for boys, was extended within two years to include girls, and is for achievement in an increasingly wide range of spheres including adventurous

enterprises, rescue work and public service, study, crafts-manship and physical fitness. Nor does he restrict himself to award-winning youth, using his energies as forcefully for young drug addicts and juvenile offenders as for their more fortunate brothers and sisters higher up the socially acceptable scale.

On universities Prince Philip holds stringent, not always popular views. 'Perhaps the most important point is that for the people who go there it is a beginning and not an end in itself . . . one of the major difficulties produced by an obsession with "paper qualifications" is that they have tended to create a sort of academic hierarchy within professions and vocations. While the qualifications may be valuable in terms of scholarship, they qualify for very little else.' Despite these views or perhaps because of them, he is Chancellor of the Universities of Wales, Edinburgh and Salford and a life Governor of King's College in the University of London.

His restless energies he channels into travelling the world, sometimes with the Queen or as her special representative, sometimes in his capacity of Admiral of the Fleet, Field Marshal or Marshal of the Royal Air Force. In one year he visited Greece, Iceland, Malawi, Malta, Mexico, the Galapagos Islands, Panama and the West Indies; in another America, Canada, the Netherlands, Norway, Germany, Jamaica, Argentine, Monaco, Italy and France. Rarely are the visits just a social occasion, and his twenty-four thousand mile tour of Pacific island territories and Australia gave him the opportunity of meeting the inhabitants of parts of the Commonwealth not previously visited by the royal family.

A dedicated conservationist and wild life enthusiast, he has produced two books, *Birds from Britannia*, a collection of bird photographs taken on his voyages, and *Wildlife Crisis*, on the preservation of wild life, written jointly with the late James Fisher. Waste in any shape or form is anathema to Prince Philip. 'We can save about four

Dressage – Princess Anne allows herself a moment f reflection before this most skilled and elegant of all equestrian events at Kiev Russia, in 1973.

Again at Kiev, reflection has been replaced by action. Airborne on Goodwill.

hundred million pounds a year in imports,' he declared recently, and went on to suggest how rubbish could be converted into useful products to a far greater degree than at present practiced. Again and again he returns to science – even inventing one of his own: dontopedalogy, 'the science of opening your mouth and putting your foot in it, one I have practised for a good many years'.

The remark was a joke, but there was an uncomfortable amount of truth in it. The Prince's career has indeed been marked by clashes with those who one way or another have offended him – most notably the representatives of the press. For him the future must hold especial problems.

A man in the mid-fifties, he has in effect been doing the same job for twenty-five years. Now his eldest son is of an age to take over many of his responsibilities. It is never easy for a man of talent and undiminished energy to slip into the background, yet this, to some extent, is what he is going to have to do. At least he can congratulate himself that, however the role of the royal family and his own place within it may be modified, the changes will take place on a foundation of affection and mutual respect very different from the jealousy and acrimony that has so often prevailed in the past.

Until a wrist injury forced him to give up polo, this was one of his great delights and at Windsor it was Princess Anne who groomed his ponies for him. When as a substitute he took up carriage driving, it was not long before his daughter was learning how to handle a carriage and pair also. Like her father she is a participator, never an onlooker for long. Prince Philip taught her to swim – she could dive off his shoulders by the time she was six – and encouraged by him she was driving a bubble car on the private roads at Windsor by the time she was nine. It was all part of Prince Philip's approach to the education of his children. Princess Anne and her brothers have all gone to school, sharing routine chores and pleasures and most important of all, perhaps, the friendships which would have been impossible within the confines of a royal schoolroom. Courage, integrity, a sense of adventure: these are the qualities Prince Philip rates so highly and has tried to instil in the junior members of what his father-in-law King George VI would affectionately describe as 'the family firm'.

By no one will those qualities be more needed than Prince Charles. It is hard to define a reigning dynasty but even on the most generous calculations one can only discover some twenty-four or twenty-five in the world today, many of them are in peril and the wastage is such that almost no year goes by without the disappearance of a King or an Emperor, a Sultan or an Emir. In an age of such

violent transition, with monarchy apparently so unfashionable a concept, can the British royal family survive indefinitely? Will there ever be a King Charles III? We may think we know the answer, but who can predict with confidence by what we will be confronted in ten or twenty years? What is at least certain is that the future of the British monarchy depends to a great part on the impression which Prince Charles makes upon his future subjects. No individual can reverse the flow of history but he can do a great deal to direct it, or at least to swim with it rather than to drown by battling against the current. This is the challenge that Prince Charles now faces. That he himself recognises and accepts the challenge was well shown when he declared: 'The demands have altered, but I am determined to serve and to try as best I can to live up to those demands whatever they might be in a rather uncertain future.'

Realising how exacting a life their son must face, the Queen and Prince Philip determined to give him as relaxed and happy a springboard for the future as it was possible to plan. But this could not be done by cosseting. Prep school; Gordonstoun – not the easiest place in which to find your royal feet; and Timbertop in Australia – 90 degrees in the shade, fly-infested expeditions and the title of Pommy basket – all contributed to give him a non-Palace view of life. This was necessary to balance the princely trappings to which he was born.

On the Queen's accession in 1952 he became Heir Apparent and Duke of Cornwall, the title assumed by the eldest son of the Sovereign under a charter of 1337. Six years later, at the age of nine and a half, he was created Prince of Wales. From that time on he has been learning with growing success how to walk the tightrope on which society has placed him.

He travels widely, enjoys life in the services, particularly in the Navy, works hard because that's the way he wants it, and like his father, expects his men to do the same. Born

*t the Shah of Iran's
nquet at Persepolis
lebrating 2,500 years of
e Persian dynasty.*

to an acceptance of duty he recognises the necessity for discipline in his own life before he can demand it in others, and his courage is without question. His sense of humour is lively, his courtesy immediate. Interviewed one day when he was very tired, he told his interviewer, 'If I fall asleep you must forgive me. And wake me . . .'

He has his own home in Kent; Chevening House, a seventeenth century mansion left to the nation by Lord Stanhope in 1967. The estate is managed by trustees and no public money is involved. At the Palace his suite on the second floor overlooking the Mall is a blend of traditional and contemporary furnishing with additional decor by way of his Malta paintings, Eskimo carvings, scale model of the Apollo spacecraft and a 24-carat gold moon complete with craters, the work of Louis Osman who designed his Investitute coronet.

Prince Charles is very aware of his responsibilities to Wales and, before the ceremony at Caernarvon Castle, was acutely conscious that he was not altogether welcome. Yet, following his stay at the University of Wales, there were ten thousand applications for the six hundred and seventy places available, and after the Investiture a Fishguard hotelier expressed the view that the Prince was the very person to take the country by the scruff of its neck and put it back on its feet. The mayor of Caernarvon, critic turned enthusiast, observed: 'You could put a suit of armour on that boy and send him to Agincourt. I reckon he's the ace in the royalist pack.' A substantial advance on the bomb threats, placarding and Nationalist rumblings of only a few weeks before.

Princess Anne's initiation into the family firm took place a year after leaving Benenden, the school in Kent where she gained six O-levels, two A's and a reputation for being always in a hurry. Her eighteenth birthday present from her parents had been a Rover 2000, the number plate – obtained from a United Dairies milkfloat in Ealing – a present from the 14th/20th Hussars of which she is

Colonel-in-Chief. Some few months later she kept her first public engagement by presenting the traditional leeks to the Welsh Guards on St David's Day. 'Let Anne be allowed to bloom on her own', a magazine had pleaded. She did just that.

Volatile, extrovert, impulsive, she drove a London bus, a police car on the testing ground and a fifty-six ton Chieftain tank. She opened youth centres, danced in Paris, launched a tanker, became President of the Save the Children Fund, Commandant-in-Chief of the St John Ambulance and Nursing Cadets, and Patron of the Riding for the Disabled movement. She held her own off-the-cuff press receptions at the Palace which were highly successful; wore trendy clothes and more important, Wore Hats. They became a talking point in trains, supermarkets and every woman's magazine.

1973, and the wedding of the year. Princess Anne with Captain Mark Phillips and the royal family on the balcony at Buckingham Palace.

In 1970 she accompanied the Queen and Prince Philip on their Captain Cook bicentenary tour of Fiji – where wolf whistles followed her departure – Tonga, New Zealand and Australia. She visited Germany in June, paid a three-day visit in July to Washington and returned to Germany in September to present the Queen's Colour to the RAF Germany on behalf of the Queen. A year later Prince Charles accompanied her to Kenya and in Nairobi they saw the work of the Save the Children Fund from the ground floor. A film for the television programme *Blue Peter* was made with her active co-operation; they were entertained by President Kenyatta, visited Treetops in the Aberdare Game Reserve and took time off to go snorkel diving in the teeming waters off the east coast of Africa. It was a good beginning to a good year.

That August Anne celebrated her twenty-first birthday, then cut short her Scottish holiday to compete in the Eridge Horse Trials. She was beaten by Mark Phillips, a Lieutenant in the Queen's Dragoon Guards, but went on to win the European Championship and become the highly popular choice of BBC Sports Personality of the Year. Less than twelve months later, her engagement was announced following a family weekend at Balmoral, and Londoners cheered at the station when Anne, Mark and their respective Labradors, Flora and Moriarty, stepped off the morning train.

But those cheers were as nothing compared with the reception given when, newly married, they emerged smiling from Westminster Abbey on that golden autumn day in 1973. A Princess and a commoner had fallen in love, married and if the fates were kind would live happily ever after. It was just the tonic we needed. Briefly, for a fleeting moment, all *was* well with the world, theirs and ours, and the shining warmth of their happiness lit the drabbest corners of a weary, crisis-ridden Britain.

There are nine and a half years difference between Anne and her second brother Andrew, born on the 19th February

1960, but they have much in common. Both have the
Mountbatten temperament, the restless impatience of their
father, his skill with words, his humour and highly indi-
vidualistic approach. Andrew is tough and independent.
Anyone who rags him at Gordonstoun or at home gets as
good as he gives. Football, skating, climbing, gliding, he
hurls himself into anything and everything with the same
enormous energy and enthusiasm.

Prince Edward, fair-haired, blue-eyed, a gift for the
colour cameras, is four years younger. Quieter than
Andrew, he's a great reader with a probing, sensitive mind
and innate sense of dignity. But he has his aunt's gift of
mimicry and love of music and his grandmother's sense of
fun. He inherited Andrew's pony Valkyrie when he was

LEFT
A refreshing ice for Prince Edward and Lady Sarah Armstrong Jones between events at Badminton.

RIGHT
Resembling strikingly his great-great-grandfather Edward VII – Prince Edward at the Royal Windsor Horse Show in 1970.

BELOW
Playtime for a Prince 1968.

not quite three and has been riding ever since. Early dreams of becoming an astronaut have given way to driving the Landrover, and, encouraged by his grandmother on Scottish holidays, he has become an early and accomplished fly-fisher. In waist-high waders and squashed-in hat, the Queen Mother instructs him in the art in which she is highly skilled, and they spend long tranquil hours in the Dee together.

The Queen Mother is probably the member of the family most generally loved and unequivocally respected. The place which she occupies in the nation's affection is shown by the way she is almost invariably referred to as 'The Queen-Mum', a title reflecting the warmth and sympathy which she radiates herself and thus inspires in others. She performs to a marvel the trick which many aim for yet few achieve, of being simultaneously homely and regal. She has the common touch. Leaving a grandiose ceremony in St. Paul's Cathedral she, Prince Philip and the Lord Mayor jostled apologetically for position as they tried to sort themselves into the precise formation which protocol dictated. 'Let's go down together,' suggested the Queen Mother. 'It's so much more sensible.' It was and they did.

At seventy-six she still leads an active life, bearing her share of the terrifying burden of public engagements which the royal family is duty bound to carry. Still keeping about one hundred and fifty engagements a year, she travels by helicopter to save time, is an authority on wine, particularly champagne, whistles charmingly, and has an endearing reputation for unpunctuality. She can laugh uproariously at a Feydeau farce, particularly enjoys eating out of doors and, serenely ignoring diet sheets and calories, indulges a taste for scones and cherry jam.

On Noel Coward's seventieth birthday the Queen Mother gave a luncheon party to which he was invited. Unhappily she went down with 'flu and he received an apologetic message concluding: 'My two daughters will understudy me'. They did, and it was at this luncheon that he heard of his proposed knighthood. Every August 4th is a signal for an avalanche of presents, flowers and thousands of birthday cards to pour into the Queen Mother's home. On her seventy-fifth birthday, as the Coldstream Guards approached Clarence House on the way to the Changing of the Guard, their band broke into a jubilant rendering of 'Happy Birthday to You' – a gesture which must have made her day.

Scotland is a special source of joy, whether at Birkhall, her white-walled Jacobean house on the Balmoral estate, often shared with Princess Margaret and her family, or two hundred miles north at her remote and windswept Castle of Mey. Here, living rooms are warmly furnished with flower-patterned chintzes, deep comfortable chairs and favourite paintings; and bedrooms are decorated in soft corals and aquamarines, colours echoed in carpets, curtains and towels in the tiny accompanying bathrooms fitted into the circular turrets of the Castle. This is the home where she found solace after the death of George VI, where walled gardens stem borders overflowing with old-fashioned flowers, and grassy walks lead down to the sea and seal-haunted beaches.

But she is never allowed to stay away too long, and her engagement diary has few gaps from January to January. Her philosophy is as uncluttered as her highland hills – 'If you're interested in people, you can't be bored; if you're not bored you won't be tired' – and fatigue, unlike cherry jam, is a luxury which she does not permit herself. Her contribution to the happiness and stability of the royal family has been and remains immense.

7. The Family Firm – 2

'It upsets me said the prince lapping up his strawberry ice all I want is peace and quiet and a little fun and here I am tied down to this life he said taking off his crown being royal has many painful drawbacks.'

There must be many occasions when the royal family share the feelings of nine-year-old Daisy Ashford's prince in *The Young Visiters* and bewail those 'painful drawbacks'. Yet in the fifty-seven years since she wrote her small masterpiece, life has changed considerably within the royal households and the Court itself. Princess Margaret pioneered the way when she married the official photographer at the wedding of her friends Lady Anne Coke and Colin Tennant – Anthony Armstrong-Jones. He introduced her to an entirely new world of writers, artists, actors and craftsmen. He gave supper parties for her in his tiny basement home beneath his studio in the Pimlico Road and at his second home overlooking the Thames at Rotherhithe, with its bustling panorama of tugs and barges, cranes and warehouses and flotillas of grubby but elegant swans. They dined together unrecognised in Soho, went to the theatre and met at friends' houses. The Queen Mother invited him to Royal Lodge and when all difficulties had been smoothed away, the Princess and the photographer married, honeymooned aboard *Britannia* and returned to start a new chapter in royal circles.

1a Kensington Palace became their London address, which was not only their home but contained a study, dark-

room, secretary's office and work-room exclusively Lord Snowdon's. His study was an amalgam of photographic equipment, pictures, magazines and recording-stereo apparatus that could be switched to any room in the house. His desk, large and functional, he designed and assembled himself. The long drawing room overlooking the garden is comfortably furnished with deep sofas, a grand piano supporting a gallery of family photographs, books and magazines neatly stacked on a stool, Anthony Fry paintings and a paper-cluttered desk.

Princess Margaret shares her mother's attitude to boredom, reads widely, is a formidable mimic, loves music and longs to travel more than her schedules ever permit.

1960 : Princess Margaret and Lord Snowdon on the balcony at Buckingham Palace after their wedding in Westminster Abbey.

OVERLEAF
Wagon grandstand for the royal family, the Duke and Duchess of Beaufort and friends at Badminton Horse Trials.

President of the Royal Ballet School, she has danced with Nureyev, and her daughter, Lady Sarah, received lessons from Dame Ninette de Valois. The Princess is an inveterate collector – of silver teaspoons, delicately ornamented eighteenth-century patch-boxes, and sea-shells which she has used in her bathroom decor on glass shelves in a white painted cabinet in the centre of the room. Red walls, curtains and carpets lend immediate warmth, and light is reflected from mirrored walls and a series of blue Bristol glass bottles. In a West Country scrapyard Lord Snowdon found a Gothic pine sideboard which, painted and mirrored, has become a dressing-table with fitted basin. This, with a Gothic door and pillars, and cornice found in Hammersmith, transformed a rather uninspired bathroom into one very much of their own making. Their children – David, Lord Linley, known at school just as Linley, and his sister Sarah – both enjoy country pursuits and enthusiastically attend the horse trials at Badminton with the Queen. An invitation from her to cruise in *Britannia* is an exciting bonus to any holiday – David sharing a cabin with Prince Edward – particularly if the programme includes a visit to the Queen Mother at the Castle of Mey.

Early in 1976 what had long been the subject of private gossip moved into the public sphere when Princess Margaret and Lord Snowdon formally separated. When one considers the strains to which such a marriage is subject, the constant pressure of living one's life so largely in the public eye, the wonder is perhaps rather that so many royal marriages prove conspicuously successful, than that this particular one foundered. Certainly no one who has not experienced their way of life has any right to condemn them.

The Queen's sister, her mother, her husband, her children: these are the backbone of the family firm, the people who spring first to mind when one thinks of the royal family. At the other end of the spectrum are the hundreds, probably thousands of people who can claim

adminton Horse Trials – d laughter out of Court r the Queen, Princess nne, Captain Mark hillips, Sir John Miller d trainer Alison Oliver.

Derby Day with Princess Alexandra, Princess Anne, Prince Philip, the Queen Mother and the Queen.

some sort of kinship with the Queen. Between these two extremes lie the descendants of King George VI's brothers who are unequivocally royal yet are not expected to conduct themselves as senior members of the family; who have their own way to make in the world yet are not wholly free of the duties and privileges which surround their cousins.

The Queen Mother must often look round her always growing family and reflect how strangely history repeats itself. As the youngest child of an ancient Scottish family, she married the Duke of York. Katharine Worsley, youngest child of the squire of one of the largest estates in Yorkshire, married the Duke of Kent. For the Queen Mother, home was Glamis Castle, said to be the oldest inhabited house in the British Isles; Macbeth was a Thane of Glamis. For Katharine it was Hovingham Hall in its setting of fine lawns, magnificent beechwoods and four thousand good northern acres. Nearly two hundred years ago a writer visited the Hall and described it in detail. Today it is almost exactly the same, even to the busts on top of the library shelves. Both the Queen Mother and Katharine grew up separated from greatly loved elder brothers sent away to school, and both, happy, compassionate, out-going people, were born to an acceptance of responsibility and service to others.

Sir William Worsley as Lord-Lieutenant of the North Riding was official host of the county and the royal family when the occasion arose, and it was in this capacity that he entertained the young Duke of Kent when he was stationed at Catterick Camp. Even twenty years before, the marriage of his daughter into the royal family would have seemed extraordinary, to some perhaps improper; it was a measure of the way in which Princess Margaret's marriage had accustomed everyone to the idea of change that the announcement of the Duke of Kent's engagement caused scarcely a raised eyebrow. Certainly it has been the source of great happiness to all concerned.

Until the Duke left the service in 1976, the requirements of an army career naturally dominated the lives of the young Kents. This, however, did not stop the Duchess involving herself in the world beyond it. Amongst a long list of public appointments, she is Chancellor of Leeds University, Controller-Commander of the WRAC, President of Scarborough Cricket Festival – which must have delighted her father who was Captain and President of Yorkshire County Cricket Club – and she is deeply involved with Age Concern. When, for security reasons, the Kents left Coppins in Buckinghamshire to live in London, an away-from-it-all home took on a new significance. And if their Norfolk house is a joy to their children, the Earl of St. Andrews, Lady Helen and Lord Nicholas, with its wide skies and freedom from routine, it is an equal blessing to the Duke and Duchess of Kent.

Best Man at their wedding was the Duke's younger

brother, Michael, who has also made the Army his career, his regiment the 11th Hussars. Poor eyesight disqualified him for the Navy, his first choice, but having passed into Sandhurst he decided to learn to fly. After less than eleven hours instruction he was flying solo and is the third member of the royal family to gain a pilot's licence. Speed and machines have always fascinated him. He took the Institute of Advanced Motorists' test, is a fearless skier and has had breathtaking escapes on the bobsleigh run. With his regimental team he took part in the trans-Atlantic air race from New York's Empire State Building to London's Post Office Tower, hurtling between check-points by plane, speedboat and helicopter, relishing every second.

Princess Alexandra, sister to the Duke of Kent, is probably the royal cousin who has done most to catch the public imagination. She too married a commoner – Angus Ogilvy, younger son of the Earl of Airlie – and has remained Princess Alexandra, Mrs Ogilvy to this day. Traditionalists splutter that such a description is absurd, no Royal Highness can be a mere Mrs, but she and her husband serenely go their own way. Her home, at Thatched Lodge House in Richmond Park, presents the same blend of informality and dignity; if anyone can emulate the unique status of the Queen Mother it will perhaps be Princess Alexandra.

James, her son, is just ten days older than Prince Edward and from sharing classes in the Palace schoolroom they have shared practically everything ever since. With him now at school at Heatherdown and Angus Ogilvy leaving every day for the city, Thatched Lodge might seem a little empty if Princess Alexandra ever had time to notice it. Her life, however, is as hectic as that of most members of the royal family. Her public and her private life blend imperceptibly. Patron of over thirty widely differing organisations, including the Guide Dogs for the Blind Association and the Presidency of the Imperial Cancer Research Fund, she sits on committees, attends planning conferences, visits hospitals and homes, opens exhibitions and is back in time for tea with her daughter Marina.

From her teens she established herself as one of the most popular of our ambassadors abroad. She was seventeen when she discovered Canada – or Canada discovered her – and Australia took just twenty-four hours to claim her their own. 'Alexandra the Great', 'Our Dinkum Princess', 'Good on You, Alex!' flamed the newspaper headlines. They loved her immediate delight in what they had to show her, laughed with her when plans went awry, warmed to her gaiety and sense of humour. To her fell the task of re-opening contact with Japan after the scarring years of war. She was twenty-four. For everyone concerned it must have seemed a daunting task, but her natural tact, her

The wedding of the Duke and Duchess of Kent at York.

beauty and sincerity won the Japanese people more completely than any number of conferences or more pompous visitations. The following year Princess Chichibu, sister-in-law of the Emperor, paid a private visit to Britain; Alexandra and her husband entertained the Japanese Ambassador and his wife at Thatched House Lodge, attended Japanese dinners in London, and in 1965 visited Tokyo together. The path was open for friendship and new understanding and a visit from the Emperor and Empress to this country. Princesses, however attractive, cannot work miracles. International politics are about power, power military and power economic. In the long run the relationship between Britain and Japan will be decided by self-interest and the needs of the moment. But an individual like Princess Alexandra can still do far more than the cynics would admit to improve the atmosphere, to create a climate in which difficulties between two countries can be sympathetically considered and, with luck, eliminated. It is a contribution which should not be forgotten when balances are struck seeking to establish whether or not the royal family is worth its keep.

Thatched House Lodge is a great meeting point for friends from all over the world and dinner guests within one week included three kings – from Norway, Thailand and Greece – Elizabeth Taylor and Richard Burton and committee members from the Star and Garter Home. It is also a favourite port of call for younger members of the family and one of the first places to which Prince Richard of Gloucester took his Danish fiancée, Birgitte van Deurs.

To improve her English, Birgitte had asked her lawyer father if she might go to England and enrol in a private language-school in Cambridge. He agreed. It was 1965. Two days after her arrival she went to a tea-party and among the undergraduates she met over toast and strawberry jam was one, angular and bespectacled, introduced as Richard Gloucester. She had no idea he was the son of a Duke and it was weeks before she learnt he was in fact tenth in succession to the British throne. They met frequently though rarely by design, rather in the sharing of mutual friends some of whom, with Richard who was reading Architecture, took over a derelict house in the town and put it to rights. In jerseys and paint-stained jeans they pulled down walls to give the open-plan spaciousness they required and built a staircase from a patio in the centre of the house. Furniture included black leather settees, a basketwork swing chair hanging from the ceiling and larger than life photographs of the Beatles. Main contribution from Birgitte was frying endless sausages on an elderly stove.

Mother and son on their travels again, this time at a bazaar in Canada, the Queen most unusually wearing a trouser suit.

When her course finished she returned to Denmark, seeing Richard occasionally and writing in between while they pursued their respective careers. In 1970 she took a job at the Danish Embassy not far from Kensington Palace, and moved into a Chelsea flat with three girl friends. Richard, now in partnership in Camden Town, was living in a terraced house overlooking Regent's Park Canal. They went about together and spent week-ends at Barnwell Manor. Birgitte was introduced to Prince Charles and Princess Anne and finally to the Queen at Balmoral. Later, at a Privy Council Meeting, her Majesty gladly gave her consent to their engagement, and the ring of silver and coral typified their taste for simplicity. They were married at Barnwell village church. Prince Richard had planned to live in a converted warehouse on the Isle of Dogs, but on the death of his brother, Prince William, he moved into Kensington Palace. Alexander, Earl of Ulster, was born in 1974.

The Prince is the fourth member of the younger generation of the royal family to marry a commoner. He will not be the last. The traditional argument against such marriages has always been that it involved the royal family in British politics, that only if all his near connections married princes and princesses from inside or outside the country could the monarch contrive to stand apart from the jealousies and rivalries which marked the national scene.

There was something in it once, but nothing today, and the Queen herself, with the shining example of her father's marriage to inspire her, must welcome the change as much as anyone. No one who has observed Prince Charles's remarkably sensible attitude towards the problem can doubt that whoever he chooses to marry will prove a worthy Queen. Let us hope that he will be left in peace to make his mind up for himself without too much harrying by a press anxious to turn every casual friendship into a romance and to find potential brides wherever the Prince of Wales may chance to go.

8. To the Future

'We were going to put "God Bless the Prince of Wales" right through our special Welsh humbug rock,' said the lady in a Caernarvon sweet shop, 'but we didn't think it would be appropriate.' A pity, it might well have appealed to Charles, shortly to be invested as twenty-first Prince of Wales. One of his most likeable qualities is a lively sense of humour and he certainly needed it in those months before his investiture. As he was the first to admit: 'You can't really expect people to be over zealous about the fact of having a so-called English Prince to come amongst them.' Some were quick to point out in that spring of 1969 that what it really amounted to was a non-Welsh Prince paying homage to his Anglican mother in a ceremony staged by a Roman Catholic Duke in a largely non-conformist country required to celebrate its own subjugation at the hands of the English. Hardly a promising undertaking.

It had been decided that the Prince should spend some weeks before the investiture at the University of Wales in Aberystwyth, a seaside holiday town on the west coast. His reception was mixed. Some of the inhabitants were enthusiastic, others apathetic, yet others openly hostile. Characteristically he didn't wait for the dust of his arrival to settle before he was at the National Eisteddfod making an eloquent appeal – in Welsh – for conservation.

'In South Wales nearly an acre disappears under mine wastage every three days. I could go on until I am blue in the face and you are, I hope, aware of many of the prob-

*ince Charles ready for the
e-off. The emblem of the
d Dragon of Wales on his
ulder has now been
pted by a wing of
squadron, Yeovilton.*

lems. An enormous percentage of the population of Britain and of Wales seems to be totally unaware except when it is too late. . . .'

They loved it and from being a foreigner from over the border, he became their *cariad bach*, their little darling. Every morning at ten o'clock he drove up to the university to study Welsh history and literature and practise the language – confounding his critics by acquiring a very acceptable accent. 'No one but a gifted mimic,' commented the university registrar, 'could have learnt to pronounce it so well.'

Meanwhile Caernarvon was warming up for the festivities. Parking had to be found to accommodate thousands of cars and coaches. A local firm provided the town with five thousand pounds worth of free paint, the electricity board guaranteed free electricity for illuminations and shops were flooded with souvenirs – cuff links, cravats, coffee sets, brooches, tankards, dolls, even pie funnels.

Lord Snowdon was responsible for the Castle and the Earl Marshal, the Duke of Norfolk, as always was ultimately in charge of everything. Lord Snowdon was anxious to stage the ceremony as simply as possible, using the natural beauty of the Castle setting and a dais as the central 'theatre'. A canopy of acrylic sheets was designed to cover the dais. Twenty-five feet at the front narrowing to nine feet six at the back, it was supported by steel rods resembling lances. A scale model was tested in a wind tunnel to withstand winds of sixty miles an hour and hopefully to survive the worst the British summer might produce. Television cameras had to be placed below the skyline so that they wouldn't appear on the screen; they were eventually successfully hidden in the stands and ramparts of the Castle.

Charles I at his investiture had worn 'a mantle of crimson velvet, containing eighteen yards, edged with gold lace and furred with ermine; a kirtle or surcoat containing fourteen yards, edged and furred as before and of the same

The young Prince Charles exercising his pony in the grounds of Badminton House.

stuff; laces, tassels and buttons of silk and gold, and a girdle of silk for the nether garment; a hood and cap of estate of the same velvet, with edging and furring as before.' The twenty-first Prince could hardly be expected to wear a replica of that. Instead he wore the ceremonial uniform of Colonel-in-Chief of the Royal Regiment of Wales. The coronet of gold and platinum set with seventy-five diamonds and twelve emeralds, was a modernised version of the traditional coronet and was donated by the Goldsmiths' Company. It weighed only three pounds because it had been 'grown' in an electroplating bath by a new process.

Security arrangements in the town and along the Menai Straits were tightened as July 1st approached, and on the night of the 30th June the royal family's train from London ran into a secret siding near Bangor. They stayed there until morning when they left for Sir Michael Duff's elegant and beautiful home nearby. There weren't enough cars for everyone so the Kents arrived in his farm van. Princess

Margaret flew in by helicopter.

It was overcast and a chill wind was blowing as Prince Charles arrived at the Castle. He was greeted by a twenty-one gun salute and a fanfare from twenty-four trumpeters of the Household Cavalry grouped on the battlements. His personal banner was unfurled and he walked to the Chamberlain Tower to the singing of 'God Bless the Prince of Wales'. Minutes later, the Queen's coach arrived. Lord Plunket knocked on the Water Gate demanding an entrance in the name of the Queen, the door swung open and Lord Snowdon, bearing on an oak tray the fifteen-inch long ceremonial key weighing six and a half pounds, offered it to the Queen. 'Madam, I surrender the key of this Castle into Your Majesty's hand.' The Queen touched the great key. 'Sir Constable, I return the key of this Castle into your keeping.'

In a slim pale yellow-coloured coat designed by Hartnell and a pearl-embroidered Tudor-style hat, the Queen moved slowly towards the dais. She was followed by Officers of State, Chiefs of the Armed Services, Heralds and the Earl Marshal. The Welsh and English national anthems were sung, then Garter King of Arms was requested to bring Charles from his tower. Down the narrow steps they came, Wales Herald Extraordinary, Chester Herald, the Secretary of State for Wales, two supporting Peers with the Prince and five others bearing the insignia: a silver gilt sword, a coronet, a rod made of Welsh gold decorated with ostrich feathers, a gold ring of two dragons holding an amethyst. Lastly came Lord Harlech bearing the mantle of purple velvet trimmed with an ermine cape.

Prince pays homage to his queen and mother: the most moving moment of the vestiture. 'I Charles, Prince of Wales, do become your liege man of life and limb and of earthly worship . . .'

Bowing three times, the Prince knelt before his mother and the Letters Patent were presented by the Lord Great Chamberlain to the Queen who handed them to the Home Secretary, James Callaghan, to read. The unfamiliar unpunctuated sentences, so difficult to speak, were strangely moving:

'. . . And him Our most dear Son Charles Philip Arthur George as he has been accustomed We do ennoble and invest with the Said Principality and Earldom by girding him with a Sword and putting a Coronet on his head and a Gold Ring on his finger and also by delivering a Gold Rod into his hand that he may preside there and may direct and defend those parts To hold to him and his heirs Kings of the United Kingdom of Great Britain and Northern Ireland and of Our other Realms and Territories Heads of the Commonwealth for ever . . .'

The Prince was invested with the insignia, the coronet placed on his head by the Queen who also fastened the

Bouquet from a ballerina at the Théâtre Royale de la Monnaie, Brussels.

purple mantle about his shoulders, and the Letters Patent confirming his title re-read in Welsh. It was a simple ceremony intensified by the grey Castle walls and bright emerald turf, the gold and purple of ceremonial, the banners, uniforms and robes; and in the centre of it all on a dais empty of adornment, a Queen received the homage of her son as she had received his father's at her coronation. Kneeling before her, Prince Charles placed his hands between hers and his voice rang out clear and strong:

'I, Charles, Prince of Wales, do become your liege man of life and limb and of earthly worship, and faith and truth I will bear unto you to live and die against all manner of folks.'

As in all great ceremonies, there is one moment above all that is remembered. Here at Caernarvon Castle it was when Charles raised his head to look at the Queen and they exchanged a brief smile. It was a moment of recognition, of service, of love. A moment of truth shared through television with their people in over six million homes.

Asked once if he would like to give it all up, Prince Charles said he didn't think so. 'I feel part of the job. I have this feeling of duty towards England, towards the United Kingdom, the Commonwealth, and I feel there is a great deal I can do if I am given the chance to do it.'

His is the future, and few of his future subjects do not hope fervently that the chance may be given him. But it may be many years before he is required to succeed to the throne, before his mother dies or perhaps decides that it is time to let somebody else carry on in her stead. Though Queen Elizabeth II has reigned for almost twenty-five years she is still only a woman of fifty; active, alert and fully capable of carrying on for as long as she deems fit. Her great-great-grandmother after all ruled for sixty-three years and died at the age of eighty-one, and who would have dared tell *her* that she had reigned too long?

And what can one say about the twenty-five years during

OVERLEAF
Miles of smiles in the first ever walkabout, New Zealand, 1970.

which Elizabeth has ruled over us? They have not been happy ones for Britain. Racked by economic crises; slipping inexorably in the league tables of the world's powers; sloughing off the last shreds of her empire; torn by dissension in Ireland, demands for devolution in Wales and Scotland: it is not a picture that any patriot can view with satisfaction. The Queen, of course, is not to blame; nor are her people disposed to blame her. As Sir Winston Churchill once remarked: 'A great battle is lost: Parliament turns out the Government. A great battle is won – crowds cheer the Queen.' But has the monarchy been afflicted by the encircling gloom or has it contrived to remain immune; a memory of better things and a promise of hope for the future? Or is it just becoming more and more irrelevant, a picturesque anachronism useful for attracting tourists but playing no significant part in the minds and hearts of the people?

Perhaps the Jubilee will help provide the answer. If this epoch in the history of the monarchy is allowed to pass almost unnoticed; if the arguments of cheese-paring Treasury officials prevail and they whittle the whole affair down to the level of a parish fête; if the people of the Commonwealth make it plain that they feel themselves very little if at all concerned: then indeed one may question the role of the royal family in the 1970s. But if there is a mighty swell of loyalty; if the people pour into the streets once more to greet their Queen; if from all over the world flows in the acclamation: then we who believe that the monarchy is still a living force and a great national asset will feel ourselves amply justified. In a curious way the monarchy is not unlike Tinkerbell in Barrie's *Peter Pan*: if you believe in it, it thrives; if you do not, it has no reason to exist and quietly dies. In 1977 the British people will have their chance to show that they believe in Queen Elizabeth II and ask no better than that she should continue to reign over them.

Certainly the Queen herself has successfully overcome the challenges with which she was confronted twenty-five years ago. She has established herself as a figure of authority, has indeed earned herself the right 'to be consulted, to encourage and to warn'. If there were any doubts they should be stilled by the words of Mr. Wilson at his farewell banquet in 10 Downing Street. He would advise his successor, he said, not to be taken in by the distinction which Bagehot drew between the Crown as the 'dignified' part of the constitution and the government as the 'efficient' part. 'While the executive hopes it is efficient, though making small claim to dignity, the dignified component can lay strong claim to efficiency.' If his successor had any sense, he went on, he would 'do his homework before his audiences, and read all his telegrams and Cabinet committee papers in time'. Otherwise he would find his ignorance quickly exposed and, in the nicest possible way, be made to feel a bit of a fool. The Queen,

Welcome to Suva, where two-thirds of the population are Indian but all are proudly Fijiian.

in short, knew her job thoroughly and must be taken seriously.

Through all his time as Prime Minister, Mr. Wilson concluded, 'I have enjoyed your manifold kindness, understanding and trust. For all of these I am profoundly grateful.' Jubilee Year gives the people of the British Commonwealth a chance to say that they are grateful too. Queen Elizabeth's forebears have been upon the throne for more than nine hundred years. They have seen the turmoil of the Middle Ages, the renaissance under the Tudors, the growth of the greatest Empire the world has ever known, and now, its disintegration. The present is dark, the future uncertain, but we will face it the more confidently if we stand together. 'I am your anointed Queen,' Elizabeth I told her parliament. '. . . I thank God I am endowed with such qualities that if I were turned out of the Realm in my petticoat I were able to live in any place in Christendom.' Queen Elizabeth II could make the same boast but neither she nor her mighty namesake would ever have abandoned the country that they were proud to rule. Nor, I firmly believe, will her people ever wish her to do so. 'Our institutions,' went on Mr. Wilson 'and especially the constitutional monarchy are more firmly established, based on a stronger popular backing and indeed affection, than at any time in this century.'

Let this Jubilee be a sign that the Queen and country together will overcome the difficulty of today and build a Britain prosperous, united, and able to play the part in the world which its talents and its history demand.

Celebrating their Silver Wedding Anniversary in November 1972, the Queen and Prince Philip arrive at Temple Bar, gateway to the City of London.

SOME EVENTS FROM THE QUEEN'S DIARY

February 6	1952	Death of King George VI
March 24	1953	Death of Queen Mary
June 2	1953	Coronation of Queen Elizabeth II
December	1953 ⎫	Visit to New Zealand
January	1954 ⎭	
Feb–March	1954	Visit to Australia
April	1954	Visit to Ceylon and India
May 15	1954	Return of the Queen and the Duke of Edinburgh from Commonwealth tour
June	1955	State Visit to Norway
Jan–Feb	1956	Visit to Nigeria
June	1956	State Visit to Sweden
February	1957	State Visit to Portugal
April	1957	State Visit to France
May	1957	State Visit to Denmark
October	1957	Visit to Canada, and State Visit to United States
October 21	1957	The Queen addresses the United Nations
March	1958	State Visit to The Netherlands
June–July	1959	Visit to Canada
June 26	1959	Opening of St Lawrence Seaway
February 19	1960	Birth of Prince Andrew
May 6	1960	Marriage of Princess Margaret
Jan–Feb	1961	Visit to India, Pakistan and Nepal
March	1961	State Visit to Iran
May	1961	State Visit to Italy and the Vatican
June 8	1961	Marriage of the Duke of Kent
Nov–Dec	1961	Visits to Ghana, The Gambia and Sierra Leone
Feb–March	1963	Visit to New Zealand and Australia
April 29	1963	Marriage of Princess Alexandra
March 10	1964	Birth of Prince Edward
October	1964	Visit to Canada
February	1965	State Visits to Ethiopia and Sudan

May	1965	State Visit to Germany
Feb–March	1966	Visit to West Indies – tour of Caribbean Islands
May	1966	State Visit to Belgium
July	1967	Visit to Canada for Expo 67
November	1967	Visit to Malta
August 27	1968	Death of Princess Marina, Duchess of Kent
November	1968	State Visit to Brazil and Chile
May	1969	State Visit to Austria
July 1	1969	Investiture of Prince of Wales
April-May	1970	Visits to Australia and New Zealand
July	1970	Visit to Canada
October	1971	State Visit to Turkey
Feb–March	1972	Tour of Far East
May	1972	State Visit to France
May 28	1972	Death of Duke of Windsor
July	1972	Prince Richard (later Duke of Gloucester) married
August 28	1972	Death of Prince William of Gloucester
October 19	1972	State Visit to Yugoslavia
November 20	1972	Queen and Duke of Edinburgh's Silver Wedding.
Jan–July	1973	Visit to Canada
October 20	1973	Opening of Sydney Opera House
November 14	1973	Marriage of Princess Anne
January	1974	Visit to New Zealand
June 10	1974	Death of Duke of Gloucester
February	1975	State Visit to Mexico
May	1975	State Visit to Japan
July	1976	State Visit to the United States for Bicentenary Celebrations
February 6	1977	25th Anniversary of the Accession
Feb–March	1977	Visits to New Zealand and Australasia
June 7	1977	National Celebration of Silver Jubilee

Princess Victoria Adelaide
KAISER FREDERICK III
of Germany

KING EDWARD VII.
PRINCESS ALEXANDRA
of Denmark

Princess Alice
Prince Louis
of Hesse-Darmstadt

Prince Alfr
Duchess Mar
of Russia

Prince Albert Victor

KING GEORGE V.
PRINCESS MARY OF TECH

Princess Sophie
KING CONSTANTINE I
of Greece

KAISER WILLIAM II.
Augusta Victoria
of Schleswig-Holstein
Sonderburg-Augustenburg

Prince Henry
Princess Irene of Hesse

Prince William
Princess Cecilie

Prince
Frederick

Prince
Adalbert

Prince Oscar

Duchess Victoria
Louise

Prince Louis Ferdinand
Princess Kira

Prince August
William

Prince Joachim

KING GEORGE II.
of Greece

KING ALEXANDER I.
of Greece

Elaine
KING CAROL
of Roumania

Michael

KING PAUL I.
of Greece
Frederica
of Hanover

Irene
Duke of Aosta

Duke of Aosta

Katherine

KING EDWARD VIII.

KING GEORGE VI.
LADY ELIZABETH BOWES-LYON

Princess Mary (Roy
Viscount Lascelles

Princess Sophia
KING JUAN CARLOS
of Spain

Princess Irene

George Henry Hubert
Earl of Harewood

Hon. Gerald David
Lascelles

KING CONSTANTINE II.
Princess Anne Marie
of Denmark

QUEEN ELIZABETH II.
PRINCE PHILIP
of Greece

Princess Margaret
Anthony Armstrong-Jor

Princess Alexia

Prince Nicholas

Prince Paul

David Viscount Linley

Lady Sarah
Armstrong-Jone

Elaine

Christina

Felippe

Prince Charles

Princess Anne
Captain Mark Phillips